HARRISON
FORD

HARRISON
FORD

by
Ethlie Ann Vare
and
Mary Toledo

Virgin

Published by
the Paperback Division of
W.H. ALLEN & Co Plc

A Virgin Book
Published in 1987
by the Paperback Division of
W.H. Allen & Co Plc
44 Hill Street, London W1X 8LB

Copyright © 1987 Ethlie Ann Vare and Mary Toledo

Typeset by Phoenix Photosetting, Chatham
Printed in Great Britain by
Anchor Brendon Ltd, Tiptree, Essex

ISBN 0 86369 196 X

This book is dedicated to

The Garcia and Medina family, without whom my
career would have remained just a dream – *Mary*

and

Russell Alexander Vare, who makes it all worthwhile –
Ethlie

Photographs courtesy of:

Russell C. Turiak, Ron Galella, Lazic/Sipa Press,
Pinson/Sipa Press, Villard/Sipa Press, Vaughan/Sipa Press,
Photo Trends, Star File

Contents

Acknowledgements

The authors would like to thank the many people whose help made this book possible: Beth Dubus Michel, for editorial assistance; Madeleine Morel and Karen Moline, for starting the ball rolling; the clerks of the Margaret Herrick Film Library, for their knowledge and kindness; Warner Bros. Pictures and A & M Records for their co-operation. We especially thank those who sat still for personal interviews: Howard Becker, Doug Rowe, David Somerville, Ion Harris, Jan Jackson, and Sergio Mendez. Thanks to Craig Modderno, for trying; to Bill Asumi, for pointing the way; to Beth Nussbaum, for understanding; to Tom Russen, for lending a hand; and to the Gonzales family, for sharing their collection. Without the support and assistance of Carla Toledo, Benny Garcia and John Hunt, none of this would have been possible. And, most of all, the authors would like to thank each other, for ensuring that each of us survived this.

Chapter One

The Early Years

Some men are born to greatness, some men have greatness thrust upon them – and some sort of back into it by a combination of accident and perseverance. Harrison Ford became a star unintentionally: he really only wanted to be a decent actor. His personal life became a matter of public interest mostly because he continually insisted that there was nothing very interesting about it. He refuses to talk about himself because he says there's really not much to talk about.

'Our culture's interest in actors' personal lives and opinions is just mythicalization and bullshit,' decreed Ford. Of course, he's wrong. Actors are our culture's representatives, the vehicle through which people express their beliefs, ideals, hopes and dreams. That twenty-foot-high face on the silver screen is an alter-ego for everyone in the audience. And when the big mug is a heroic Indiana Jones or Han Solo, or a sensitive John Book or Rick Deckard, the audience *does* want to know something about the man behind the face. Because we want to see something of ourselves in him.

Which is why Harrison Ford's very ordinariness – a hero born out of the most mundane surroundings – is particularly appealing. Because if Harrison Ford can be Indiana Jones, anyone can. (Amazingly, Ford had already been Han Solo three times and Indiana Jones twice when a consumer survey showed that only one in five Americans could put a name to his photograph. Everyman is Anyman.)

Harrison Ford's early life was chillingly normal. He grew up with screen heroes like Humphrey Bogart and James Cagney, but he didn't emulate them. The big movie hit the year he was born was *Mrs. Miniver*. The nation was embroiled in a war he was too young to notice. He left college just before the student movement exploded. The Chicago of his childhood boasted no bootleggers shooting it out on street corners. So why does this man embody every myth of Thirties and Forties hard-boiled heroism, evoking images of gangland 'tecs, war-weary battle aces and freelance soldiers of fortune? Goodness knows he doesn't come by it naturally.

It's just acting.

Harrison Ford was born on July 13, 1942, the first child of an Irish-Catholic father and Russian-

Jewish mother. They named their son after his maternal grandfather, Harrison Needleman, a vaudevillian who left the stage for steady work on the Brooklyn streetcar line. Harrison and his younger brother Terence spent their formative years in the pleasant, suburban communities of Park Ridge and Morton Grove, Illinois. For Harrison, life held few worries.

It was a comfortable, middle-class existence; Harrison Ford was cushioned from the blows of harsh reality. He was born too late to suffer want in the Great Depression, and too soon to fight in World War II. His mid-Western upbringing was not unlike the nostalgic idyll of mythical 'Pleasanton' or 'Centerville' that today's baby-boomer directors try to recreate in celluloid. Although he wasn't very active in sports, Harrison did conform to the macho ideals of the era by playing some baseball and spending a lot of his free time tinkering with cars. As a teenager, Ford got a summer job as a nature counsellor at a Boy Scout camp, where he spent a lot of free time catching and collecting snakes. (That's right: Indiana Jones' morbid fear of snakes was just make-believe.)

'I was a loner type,' Ford once recalled. 'I didn't know what I wanted to do when I was a kid.' Oddly, he was not one of the many outcasts-turned-superstars whose bittersweet childhood memories always include long afternoons at the local Bijou. 'I didn't spend much time at the movies,' he once said. 'I'm not a scholar of Bogart's mannerisms –

and I miss a lot of the references that people like Spielberg and Lucas toss around.'

Movies – much less acting – may have been the last thing on young Harrison's mind, but showbiz was already in his blood. Not only was granddad a player on the old burlesque stage, but his father worked as a radio actor before settling down to a career in advertising. (He was lauded for his use of time-lapse photography to pitch Parkay margarine.) Today, the senior Ford still works as a 'voiceover' artist in commercials – although it was his son's notoriety, not his own, that made the Fords' 45th wedding anniversary fit material for a *Life* magazine layout.

At the Graham Stuart Elementary School in Chicago, Harrison received good grades, and his teachers remarked that he was interested in learning. But, during his high school years at Main East Township in Des Plaines, Harrison's grades started to take the plunge.

'I thought of education only as a tool for success,' Ford explained to *Seventeen* magazine. But, even though his ardour for education was minimal, Harrison went ahead and enrolled in college.

It wasn't until he entered Ripon College – a private liberal arts institution in central Wisconsin – that things started to change in Ford's life. He majored in philosophy and minored in English and was, not to put too fine a point on it, a totally average student. 'I wouldn't call him a scholarly person, but he wasn't a problem by any means,' recalls Ion Harris, secretary to the Dean at Ripon. 'He was no genius, but he did well in the subjects that interested him.'

When, during his junior year, he was forced to choose an elective class, he stuck the pin in 'drama.' As Ford described it, 'I was trying to get my grade average up and meet some girls.'

At first, Harrison didn't care much about the quality of his performance in drama class; he was mostly concerned about getting it over with. But, after taking a few courses, he discovered that being onstage, saying lines written by (and for) other people, helped him overcome his self-proclaimed shyness.

'When I first started acting,' Ford said, 'the main satisfaction came from conquering the fear of actually getting up and doing it.' Then, he said, 'I began to experience the fun of it.' It was, he told *GQ* magazine, 'the first time I really remember having any significant ambition to do anything.' But even when he began to take seriously the idea of maintaining a career as an actor, 'I never had any ambition further than having enough work. I never imagined a situation where I would worry about the *quality* of work. That's come more lately.'

Even at the beginning, Ford looked at acting in a completely practical manner. Today, the physical job of acting is priority number one: having the work and doing it in a professional, craftsmanlike manner. The concept of stardom and celebrity is a poor second.

Ford became good friends with his drama class instructor, Richard Bergstrum, who has since died. In part due to Bergstrum's approval and enthusiasm, Harrison began to consider seriously devoting himself to acting as a profession. Ion Harris, who stills runs the Dean's office, recalls: 'He was very close to the professor who taught drama classes. Once we had a fire, and I remember Harrison running from the building, carrying out this man's books and records. Tears were just running down his cheeks. He was very, very upset that this was happening. I'll never forget that.'

The dean's secretary recalls Ford as being an outgoing person. 'He had many friends, and he belonged to one of our fraternities, Sigma Nu. He was very good friends with our dean of men, David Harris; I'd see him quite often chatting with him.' Dean Harris evaluated Ford as certainly bright enough to do a fine job, scholastically, but says he just 'didn't have his heart in it.'

Just three days prior to the Ripon graduation ceremonies, Ford was informed that he would not be receiving a degree with his classmates. This was due, Ford himself said, to the fact that he 'slept through my senior year.' The unfortunate news was received with chagrin by Harrison's parents, who had rented a motel room for the ceremony.

What Ford seemed to lack was direction. Here he was, spending four years of his life immersed in two subjects which he felt would have no bearing on his ability to make a living once out-side of the academic womb. Long before his senior year was up, he simply stopped attending classes. But Ripon did have a positive impact on his life in the long run. It was here that he met Mary Louise Marquardt – who did go ahead and graduate, with honours – whom he married after the 1963 spring semester. And, by the time he left, he had some good experience under his belt in collegiate theatrical productions.

One of Harrison's favourite student roles was as Mr. Antrobus – complete with a pillow wrapped around his stomach – in Thornton Wilder's *The Skin of Our Teeth*. It was, he said, that one appearance that first made him realize that acting was something he could *do*. After school was over, he went ahead and joined the William's Bay repertory company's summer stock season, performing in five shows over a period of three months – musicals, drama, everything – on the shores of Lake Geneva, Wisconsin. For extra money, he took a job cooking in a yacht anchored on the lake. The fact that he didn't know how to boil an egg was something he omitted to tell the owner.

One stage performance he would rather forget happened at the Belfry Theatre, druing a play-house production of Tennessee Williams' *Night of the Iguana*. Ford got a case of stage fright, and forgot his lines. 'I learned in public, and I made a lot of mistakes along the way,' laughed Ford. 'They're on television late at night! But I'm the

13

kind of person who learns from experience; I don't learn from books.'

It didn't take Harrison long to realize that Wisconsin was not exactly hopping with major motion picture studios and big-name directors; he decided that it was time to try his luck on either the east or the west coast. Which one would he choose? He vowed to base his decision on the flip of a coin. When it came up New York, he flipped again. Harrison figured if he were going to be miserable, poor and starving, he might as well do it in the sun as in the snow.

Harrison and Mary – whom he met in his last year at Ripon – packed up their belongings in a rattletrap Volkswagon and pointed west. They landed in Laguna Beach, about 60 miles south of Hollywood. Today, Laguna is a high-status residential and resort community. In the mid-Sixties, it was little more than a fishing village and artists' colony. Not exactly a hub of the entertainment industry, and not a place providing immediate job contacts for a newcomer with acting aspirations. 'I didn't even know the names of the major motion picture studios at that point,' said Ford years later.

Harrison took on a variety of odd jobs to support himself and his wife. He became 'assistant buyer of knick-knacks' at Bullock's department store in nearby Santa Ana. In the evening, he plied his craft at the Laguna Beach Playhouse. 'He had just moved into town, and he came down for an audition,' remembers Doug Rowe, who is still the artistic director of the Laguna Beach Playhouse. 'I cast him as Clay Wingate, the Southern soldier, in *John Brown's Body*. I played the Northern soldier opposite him.

'It was the only play he did for us,' continues Rowe. 'It was a remarkable piece. It was sold out every night for three weeks. And there was never any question in my mind that Harrison Ford had the potential to be an outstanding actor. There's an honesty to his work – an ability to get right to the heart of the line. He's a very subtle actor, and he never overplays.'

Coincidentally, that one Laguna season also began the careers of Ford's two repertory-mates, Mike Farrell (B.J. Hunnicutt in *M.A.S.H.*) and Toni Tennille (of the Captain and). 'All three of them appeared at the Playhouse that season,' says Rowe, 'and none were professionals at the time. It was an incredible season.'

It was on his way from one gig to the other that Ford – by now 6'1" and weighing about 170 pounds – got the only distinguishing mark on his otherwise unremarkable visage: a scar under his lower lip. He was driving through Laguna Canyon when he leaned over to fasten his seatbelt – and rammed into a telephone pole.

The Laguna Playhouse, though, gave him more than a few stitches. It was also there, during that production of *John Brown's Body*, that a man named Ian Bernard spotted Harrison, and saw in him that special spark that makes one actor stand out from those around him. 'He got a job right from the first play he was in,' smiles Doug Rowe. 'He's just a great actor, and that was immediately apparent.' Bernard sent Harrison over to a colleague, Billy Gordon, head of casting at Columbia Pictures. What was to occur in Gordon's office was fate . . . which is only a letter (and a dream) away from 'fame.'

Chapter Two

The Star System

The 'star system' has a long and not entirely noble history. It's a vehicle through which major motion picture studios 'groom' up and coming artists, create a persona for them and find appropriate roles (in that same studio's productions, of course) to bring the neophyte's career along. Signed as a 'contract player,' an actor or actress can only work for the studio that signed them – although big names can be 'loaned out' by the bosses for future business concessions.

To a newcomer, getting a job as a contract player seems like the biggest break in the world: guaranteed work, and the full muscle of a studio whose fondest hope is to make you a star pushing from behind. But often, joining a 'stable' of bit players turns into a frustrating dead end. In the early Sixties, the contract system was still alive in Hollywood – although exhaling its last gasp. It also had one new wrinkle: television.

In its *New Talent* programme, what Columbia Pictures had in mind for Ford (and the eleven other young men hired along with him) was slightly different from 'grooming for stardom.' As far as Ford was concerned, it was more like slave labour. In the matter of 'grooming,' studio execs weren't thrilled with Harrison's personal appearance in the first place. And, although one would be hard pressed to find anybody still willing to admit this in the harsh light of 20/20 hindsight, the fact is that Columbia didn't see even a glimmer of 'star quality' in young Harrison Ford.

In 1964, a 22-year-old Harrison Ford – wet behind the ears, and looking about 17 – was called in for his once-in-a-lifetime appointment at The Studio. He recalled that casting director Billy Gordon was 'a little, bald-headed guy,' who looked at Ford 'as if he'd discovered a snake in his soup.' Gordon's assistant (who looked 'like a racetrack tout') asked Ford his height and weight, whether he spoke any foreign languages, and if he could ride a horse. After a short round of questions and apparently unimpressive answers, Harrison received that time-honoured brush-off: 'Okay kid, thanks a lot. If we find anything, we'll let you know.' Ford considered this response tantamount to 'Don't call us, we'll call you' – which it was – and left the office, confused and discouraged.

But there's a fairy-tale ending to this story. On his way out of the building, Harrison decided to heed the call of nature before getting on the elevator. He took a quick detour to the nearest men's room and then, heading back to the lift, passed the casting director's office once again – just in time to see the man's assistant poke a nose out of the door. The assistant called Harrison back inside. 'Look,' said Gordon. 'You're not the type we're really interested in, but how'd ya like to be under contract?'

'I knew right from the beginning that if I had gone down the elevator instead of going to take a pee, it wouldn't have been worth chasing me down the street,' Harrison told the *Los Angeles Herald-Examiner* twenty years later.

Ford was signed for seven years (what was considered a 'short-term' contract) at a salary of $150 per week – 'and all the respect that that implies,' laughed Ford.

In many respects, the job of contract player resembled that of insurance salesman. Ford showed up at the studio every day in a jacket and tie, attended acting classes and ate lunch in the executive dining room. The worst part, he said, was having to submit to an endless barrage of photo layouts. Laconic Harrison wasn't particularly turned on by the glitz of photographer's lights, and his natural shyness rebelled at his being treated like a centrefold. 'Nobody even knew your name at the Studio, or cared a damn about you,' said Ford. 'I went nuts.'

Ford put up with this for a little over a year. It was no worse than modelling, certainly, and at least it gave him a change to polish his craft in acting class. And there was always a chance that he would, after all, be given a juicy part in a movie. The part he finally got offered, though, was no plum: he was to play a bellboy in the movie *Dead Heat on a Merry-Go-Round*, directed by Bernard Girard and starring James Coburn.

It wasn't a huge part; it wasn't even a medium-sized part. 'I had to say "Paging Mr Jones, paging Mr Jones," or something like that, and then James Coburn would wave me over and I'd give him a telegram,' recalled Ford. 'That was it.' Not terribly challenging, and yet the studio executives at the time told Ford that they weren't entirely pleased with his performance.

As Ford remembered it, a studio vice president – who is no longer in the business, and would probably deny this if you found him and asked – looked Ford in the eye and said: 'Sit down kid, I want to tell you a story. The first time Tony Curtis was in a movie, he delivered a bag of groceries. We took one look at him and knew he was a movie star. But you ain't got it, kid; you ain't got it. I want you to go to class and study.'

Ford reacted quizzically to the apocryphal tale of Tony Curtis, and answered the executive with his usual frankness: 'Gee, I thought you were supposed to look at him and say, "There is the grocery boy!" ' Looking back on it, Ford later explained, 'I thought I was supposed to act like a bellboy. It didn't occur to me until years later that what they wanted me to do was to act like a movie star.'

Harrison Ford received one mention in reviews for his $2 million picture: a trade publication noted that he 'came from a show business family' and was 'making his way to screen fame.' An unusually warm reception for a bit part.

Although his performance was considered average, Ford was offered parts in other Columbia movies: *Luv* in 1967 (in which he was little more than an extra), and *A Time for Killing* (also known as *The Long Road Home*) that same year, playing the small role of Lieutenant Shaffer in a Civil War drama starring his unrelated namesake Glenn Ford and George Hamilton. But it was just a matter of time before Harrison's patience would run out . . . and the studio's.

'I was very unhappy,' said Ford. He was also very uncooperative. He didn't want a catchy new name, thanks, and he didn't want his hair pompadoured like Elvis Presley's. He was very happy to be plain old Harrison J. Ford.

Harrison *J.* Ford?

The fact is, Harrison did have to change his name to work in the movies, because there was already a Harrison Ford listed by the Screen Actors Guild. Since SAG won't let two performers go around using the same moniker – to prevent credit confusion – our Harrison Ford stuck in the middle initial 'J,' and that's how he appears in his first two films.

The *other* Harrison Ford was born in 1886 in Kansas City, and worked his way up through stock theatre into the ground-breaking new business of moving pictures. One of Lasky's Famous Players, the first Ford starred with the likes of Gloria Swanson and Norma Talmadge in early silent comedies. An athletic man and a voracious reader, Ford was one of the most popular film comics of his day. He didn't retire from acting until he was in his 60s, although his prominence was minor by that time – however, before his disappearance from filmdom, he was sufficiently acclaimed to be awarded a star on the Hollywood Walk of Fame. (That's right; the 'Harrison Ford' star on Hollywood Boulevard belongs to a *different* Harrison Ford.)

'When I heard the old man had passed on,' said Ford, 'I called up SAG about it. They couldn't confirm his death, but I dropped the "J" anyway.' In fact, the first Ford had died in 1957 at the age of 73.

When Harrison J. Ford's *A Time for Killing* turned out to be a flop, it was the last straw as far as Columbia was concerned. Harrison had served 18 months of his seven-year term, and the studio was ready to release him on bad behaviour. An assistant to studio head Mike Frankovitch went up to Harrison and told him, sympathetically, that his days were numbered. 'I know your wife is pregnant,' said the assistant. 'You need the money, so I'll give you another couple of weeks.' Ford, cutting off his nose to spite his face – as performers with integrity (not to mention snot-nosed kids of 23) are wont to do – promptly told the guy where to cram the paycheques. Three days later, Ford was under contract to Universal . . . same tune, new piper.

With Universal, Ford was able to work on TV – in fact, he was able to do little else, because they didn't trust him with bigger challenges. And Ford was just as happy with that as were the powers that be, because he wanted to put in some apprenticeship time before tackling the important stuff. 'I needed a lot more experience before I was worthy of better parts,' Ford said later, 'but you still have to work over your head a little bit.'

During his time with Universal, Ford had small parts in such popular television programmes as *The Virginian*, *Gunsmoke* and *Ironside*. He did one movie, *Journey to Shiloh*, a Civil War drama that had the good manners to sink without a trace. He was in two pilots for TV series ('Thank God they weren't picked up!' Ford later sighed.) Universal loaned him out to good old Columbia to play the small part of Jake in *Getting Straight*, starring Elliott Gould. The man who wanted nothing more than steady acting work was getting it – and suddenly he recognized the drawback inherent in a constant flow of bit parts. He could suffer from terminal overexposure before ever getting a major role!

'I was not prepared for the disillusionment I found as an actor in the studio system,' said Ford. It was time to make a career decision. Harrison Ford was either going to walk away from the entertainment industry, or he was going to get a part that made staying worthwhile. The decision ended up being made by the controversial director Michelangelo Antonioni – on a cutting room floor.

The youth-oriented flick *Zabriskie Point* focused on a couple of teen rebels who were making a statement about the negative influence sex and wealth had on Sixties' society. The project was one of the rare films in the era to utilize a rock 'n' roll soundtrack (now all but *de rigueur* in the industry), and featured the music of the Rolling Stones, the Grateful Dead and Pink Floyd. Ford was originally to carry a minor sub-plot in the film – a sub-plot that director Antonioni eventually decided to edit out entirely.

Looking back, it was just as well Ford wasn't associated with the movie. A monumental flop, *Zabriskie Point* is best remembered for the director's massive ego (he repainted Death Valley, because the real colours weren't good enough for him) and the fact that all involved in the production barely escaped being prosecuted for violating the Mann Act. (Nude scenes were shocking back then, and transporting underage actors across state lines to have mock-sex was almost a Federal offence.)

Zabriskie Point was an all-around jinx. Star Mark Frechette ended up joining a religious cult, and later going to prison; co-star Daria Halprin has never been heard from professionally again. And Harrison Ford, never even appearing on-screen, decided to bow out of acting altogether.

Chapter Three

Getting Away From It All

A disillusioned Harrison, his pregnant wife and their young son, Ben, were living quite simply in a small, wood-frame house up in the hills above the famed Hollywood Bowl. Ford was becoming convinced that the movie industry would never guarantee him a sufficiently steady pay-cheque to support his growing family; it was time to leave the business for something stable. He decided upon carpentry, since he 'had the right clothes for it' and had been doing a lot of busying around while rebuilding the house. ('I remember once,' says Ford's Laguna Beach buddy, Doug Rowe, who had been keeping in touch with the Ford family, 'that he didn't have enough money to buy the lumber he needed to finish remodelling the place. He was really struggling.') Carpentry as a profession, though, seemed an unlikely choice –

Harrison knew less about woodcraft than he did about theatre craft.

But just as Harrison took it upon himself to learn to be a good actor or a competent ship's cook, he determined to become a good carpenter. He went back to the old study habits he had picked up (albeit not used very much) in college, and started learning his new trade from books.

Ford became an habitué of the Encino public library, where he loaded himself up with texts on carpentry. His first professional assignment was a lucky break: a juicy, $100,000 contract to build a home-recording studio for A&M Records artist Sergio Mendes (of Brasil '66), a South American composer who lived three blocks away from the suburban library.

'I'd be standing on Mendes' roof with a textbook in one hand and a hammer in the other,' recalled Ford. Not only was he making better money than he ever did as an actor but, ironically, the experience would later turn one of his finest scenes into such a realistic piece of construction (literally), that it's fair to say his carpentry helped earn him an Oscar nomination. Life is strange.

'A friend of mine had recommended him for the job,' recalls Mendes. 'He seemed to know what he was talking about, even though he had no papers or anything that indicated he was a carpenter. He seemed to take a lot of care in what he was doing, and I like that. I hate to use the word "perfectionist," but he was very careful and neat and did a great job.

'During his break time, he would read books about carpentry, as well as film scripts. He told me that he wanted to be in the movie business.

'He worked here for more than six months,' continues Mendes. 'The studio came out gorgeous, with stained glass we got from a mausoleum in Tennessee, and hand-crafted hardwood floors. It was a fantastic job – we still use the studio today.

'Ford was a very quiet fellow, who didn't socialize much. His wife used to come over and bring him food on his lunch break. He didn't talk much, that one. Very self-possessed, and quietly proud of his accomplishments. A guy who knew what he was doing, and took care of business.'

Ford said that carpentry was the best thing that could have happened to him. He learned the value of money and work, and he was making enough to afford the luxury of turning down roles – roles which he felt might be fatal to his nascent career. 'It saved my life to have another way of making a living,' he once said. 'Carpentry gave me the possibility of choice, the ability to turn down roles.' Harrison turned down 90 per cent of the acting opportunities that dribbled in.

'I didn't want to do episodic TV anymore, because I was afraid I'd burn myself out before I got a chance to do any decent feature films. Besides, I was too young. I was 24 and looked 19.' At the same time, though, 'I never gave up the ambition to be an actor. I was always available for something really good.'

Singer/actor David Somerville (you may recall him as the lead vocalist on the Diamonds' million-seller, *Little Darlin'*) lived next-door to Ford at the time, and remembers Ford as a good friend, co-operative neighbour and not a bad carpenter. In fact, says Somerville, Ford helped keep his own little house from falling off the Hollywood Hills.

'This is a great part of town,' says Somerville. 'We have a direct view of the Hollywood sign. It's really very rustic-feeling. I bought this house from two old actors who had lived in it for 41 years – she passed away in 1973, and he went into the screen actors' old folks' home. Oliver Hardy once lived here, too.

'Harrison Ford lived next door,' continues Somerville. 'It was what you'd call his dues-paying period, before he became a *Star Wars* star. When I discovered that this house was beginning to slide down the hill because of geological insufficiencies, he drew a plan for me and helped me build what we naturally named the Ford Foundation. He actually came over here at 6.30 in the morning to start the job. I later reciprocated in his home with the Somerville Kitchen, which isn't half as catchy. The old Harrison house is now occupied by David Carradine.'

Carpentry instilled in Ford the work ethic and a self-discipline that he felt he lacked – both in acting class and in the college classroom. He took pride in his work, and stuck with a project until it was done. It gave him an eye for detail; now he finds it difficult to sit still and keep quiet about script additions and deletions, because the habit of perfectionism is just too strong.

'Acting is basically like carpentry,' Ford once mused aloud. 'If you know your craft, you figure out the logic of a particular job and submit yourself to it. It all comes down to detail.'

He expanded the correlation in an interview with the actor's trade magazine, *DramaLogue*: 'There's a real simple-minded analogy,' he said. 'You have to have a logical plan. You have to perceive it from the ground up. You have to lay a firm foundation. Then, every step becomes part of a logical process.' Ford said he gets so involved in his thought patterns now that he can't even distract himself when taking a break from a shoot; he finds himself 'staring at walls, or walking around and bumping into my trailer.'

Today, Ford occasionally utilizes his carpentry expertise to make hand-crafted furnishings for his own home. In the early Seventies, it was a way to put food on the table for Mary, Willard and Ben. (Ford didn't really name his two sons after the killer rats in the movie *Ben*; it wasn't made until 1972.) He became something of a 'celebrity handyman,' taking carpentry assignments from the likes of James Caan, Richard Dreyfuss and James Coburn.

Things were going well for Ford in carpentry, and things were also beginning to look interesting in the acting department.

In 1972, Ford was approached by Fred Roos,

one of the only Columbia-era friends in the business he had remained close to. An associate of up-and-coming director/producer Francis Ford Coppola, Roos was 'on loan' to Coppola's friend George Lucas, who was trying to get financing for a project he had in mind about his memories of high school in Modesto, California. Coppola, who had met Lucas when a neophyte George used to hang out on the set of Francis's *Finian's Rainbow* project and later hired him to work on *Rain People*, was lending his name – and his assistant – to Lucas to help with fundraising and administration. It was Roos, the man responsible for placing Ford (temporarily) in *Zabriskie Point*, who offered Harrison Ford the small role of drag racer Bob Falfa in *American Graffiti* – at Universal Pictures, of all places. (Columbia had turned down the project as fiscally unreliable.)

It was a little picture by Hollywood standards – a budget of only $750,000 (industry average today is over $7 million) that resorted to such cost-cutting measures as offering extras a chance to win prizes instead of giving them a pay-cheque. More money went for the period hot-rods: $25 a day per car. The cast of relative newcomers was chosen after cattle-call auditions that brought 150 hopefuls a day through the doors.

Part of the reason *American Graffiti* was such a hit was its soundtrack – one of the first to string pop songs end on end rather than simply contract an instrumental score. Although Universal executives tried to convince Lucas to cut the soundtrack down to five or six tunes, the director was adamant, and the *American Graffiti* album sold 100,000 copies in its first two weeks of release. Lucas had bought the rights to 42 songs from 1955–1962 for $80,000. That's less than today's savvy rockers would demand for 'synch' rights on a single hit tune; Columbia had been convinced that song rights would run $500,000 alone.

One song that never made it onto the soundtrack, however, was Rodgers and Hammerstein's *Some Enchanted Evening*, which Ford's character sang – off-key – in a scene that Harrison had ad-libbed. Although the scene was a favourite of Lucas, neither Richard Rodgers nor the estate of Oscar Hammerstein II would sign over rights to the song for Ford's comic presentation.

The shoestring budget allowed for 28 nights (not days) of location work during June, 1972 in San Rafael and then rural Petaluma, California – a town that reminded Lucas of his native Modesto as it was a decade earlier. Local merchants kept their own store lights shining (at personal expense) so that the director could complete his scenes. The film was concluded with a Fifties-style sock hop party at Art Laboe's rock revival club on the Sunset Strip. 'Help us celebrate by cruising on down Sunset,' said the invitation, 'for a double Chubby Chuck and a Coke.' It was all great fun, with a spirit of camaraderie and nostalgia permeating the done-for-love project.

Who could have predicted that the darn thing

would go on to gross $117 million and earn Oscar nominations for Best Picture, Best Story, Best Editing and Best Director? *American Graffiti* instantly transformed the careers of everyone involved – everyone, that is, except Harrison Ford.

A diametrical opposite to *Zabriskie Point*, this sweet slice-of-life movie was a rabbit's foot for its cast. The star was child actor Ron Howard ('Opie' in the television series *The Andy Griffith Show*), who would go on to direct blockbuster films like *Cocoon* and *Splash*. Co-star Richard Dreyfuss would win an Academy Award in 1977 for *The Goodbye Girl*. Suzanne Somers, who had only a tiny, non-speaking role, would shortly be a prime-time television siren and household name. Charles Martin Smith, Paul Le Mat, Cindy Williams, Mackenzie Phillips, Candy Clark – no one in the cast seems to have slipped into obscurity. But, at the time, it seemed like the exception to the rule was going to be the fellow who played the evil dragster from out-of-town. Harrison Ford finished *American Graffiti* and promptly went back to carpentry.

The actors and actresses, at the time, had no idea of the film's long-range impact. Yet there was still that inkling that the project was headed for success. Cindy Williams remembers sitting next to Harrison at an early screening of the director's cut, and said he turned to her and cried 'This is great!' At the film première in May '83, however, Dale Pollock reported in his book

Skywalking that Ford slunk out of the theatre half-way through the final version, embarrassed and disappointed by his work. The critics weren't. '*American Graffiti* is one of those rare films,' wrote *Variety*, 'which can be advanced in any discussion of the superiority of film over live performance. The latter can vary from show to show, but if you get it right on film, you've got it forever.' The *Hollywood Reporter* said the film 'has a lot to say [but] it's gloriously free of pretensions.' The *Los Angeles Times* called it 'masterfully executed and profoundly affecting.'

Not at all a bad return to the big screen for Harrison Ford.

Ford was to team up with Cindy Williams again in Francis Ford Coppola's *The Conversation* – another acting job secured for him by Fred Roos. The film was a subdued and eerie piece about a professional surveillance man (Gene Hackman) and the couple he is trailing. Williams played the suspect girlfriend, walking through the critically-acclaimed (although commercially unsuccessful) movie quite unaware that events were spiralling down into a morass of paranoia – paranoia that would eventually be confirmed by grisly fate. Coppola described *The Conversation* as a 'sort of psychological horror film.' Ford played Martin Stett, 'a corporate hatchet man,' who had no personality to speak of until Ford decided to make the character a homosexual. Although the film won the Grand Prize at the Cannes Film Festival, Ford's work remained largely unnoticed.

Next, Ford played a walk-on role – a watery-eyed witness – in the 1974 television movie *The Court Martial of Lieutenant Calley*, a video response to the alleged Vietnam war crimes of US soldiers at My Lai. Respected director Stanley Kramer was at the helm, and he remembered Ford as being 'tremendously sensitive' as an actor. The film was minor, but well thought of. The same year, he took a lighter-weight project in the tele-flick *Dynasty*, which was based on the James Michener novel about 19th-century pioneers, and bore no resemblance to the popular prime-time series with the same title.

Eight years had passed since Ford gave up his status as a studio contract player. 'In those eight years,' said Ford, 'I did only four acting jobs, but three of them were good ones: *American Graffiti*, *The Conversation* and *The Court Martial of Lieutenant Calley*. After eight years, nobody thought of me as a person who had been in anything but three good films.'

Chapter Four

What Lucas Hath Wrought

It was 1976, and Harrison Ford was working on refurbishing actress Sally Kellerman's kitchen. His old buddy George Lucas, though, was working on a new, risky movie idea. It was going to be called *Star Wars: Episode IV – A New Hope*, a science fiction 'horse opera' recreating the style of old Saturday morning film serials like *Flash Gordon*. (Lucas once tried to option rights for author Alex Raymond's *Flash Gordon* itself, but discovered he had been beaten to the punch by Italian director Federico Fellini, of all people.) After Universal, who had first option, turned down the $10 million project (a decision that cost them about $250 million all told), the package was picked up by Alan Ladd Jr. at Twentieth Century-Fox. The studio wasn't happy with the title – demographic surveys proved that the word 'war' on a hoarding kept female ticket-buyers away from the theatre – but Lucas was riding on the success of *American Graffiti*, and was given a certain amount of free rein.

The year George Lucas started casting *Star Wars*, Harrison Ford had not earned the minimum $1,200 as an actor required to keep him qualified for SAG health insurance. With the new addition of second son Willard, he needed an acting job if he was going to be able to pay the medical bills. Carpentry was keeping food on the table, but Ford wanted a role to get back on the insurance rolls. In the end, ironically, it was carpentry that made possible the biggest break in his screen career. You could say that a nail nailed the deal.

Ford figured that his prior association with George Lucas would help him get at least a shot at one of the better parts in Lucas' forthcoming project, although that turned out to be far from the truth. It was his prior association with Francis Ford Coppola that got Harrison's foot in the door – not for the casting call, but for a carpentry job. Ford was hired to install an elaborate raised panel in the producer's studio office. As Ford recalled, 'I knew they were casting, and I thought it would be a bit coy to be around Francis's office being a carpenter during the day. So I did the work at night.' After pulling a few all-nighters, Ford fell behind schedule, and had to come in during the day to catch up. It turned out to be the very day that George Lucas and his friend, director Brian de Palma, decided to start running through hundreds of young unknowns for their two projects: Lucas for *Star Wars*, and de Palma for *Carrie*. 'There were guys literally everywhere,' remembered Mark Hamill, 'in age from 16 to 35.'

So here was Harrison Ford, down on his knees in the doorway of Francis Ford Coppola's office, hammering away and trying to look inconspicuous, when in walked Coppola, Lucas and actor Richard Dreyfuss. Dreyfuss is trading jokes with Coppola, and Ford is trying like hell to become invisible. He felt, he said, about the size of a pea.

As Lucas began to call in the hundreds of hopeful Han Solos, Princess Leias and Luke Skywalkers for their auditions, Ford kept his mouth shut and kept up his work on Coppola's panel. Since Lucas knew and liked Harrison's work in *Graffiti*, he asked his friend to help run lines with the potential Princess Leias. Ford didn't mind, but he did admit to feeling a bit of irritation and frustration that he was reading for a part he would never play. He had already been warned that Lucas planned to use a bevy of newcomers for the project, and had specifically discouraged the previous cast of *American Graffiti* from attending. As it turned out, Harrison's irritated crankiness won him the day.

What was most important to Lucas in his search for a trio of lead actors was not so much the prior credits, professionalism or on-screen charisma of each individual; rather, he was seeking a special interaction between the three main characters, a kind of instant chemistry. At one point, it was assumed that a black actor would play the role of Solo – actor Glynn Turman was strongly considered – an idea that later metamorphosed into the character of Lando Calrissian. Other actors considered for the part of Han included William Katt and even Nick Nolte. Lucas once said that it was Ford's self-deprecating manner combined with the 'churlish' qualities apparent from his bad mood that made him stand out from the other interviewees. But the clincher was the way he segued smoothly alongside Mark Hamill and Carrie Fisher. To Lucas, the rebel threesome were to be all or nothing.

If, for any reason, either Fisher or Hamill had been unable to take the job, we wouldn't have ended up seeing Harrison rushing to rescue, say, Jamie Lee Curtis. No, if this trio fell through, Lucas had a completely different group waiting in the wings. How would you have enjoyed *Star Wars*, do you think, with its alternate cast of Christopher Walken as Luke, Will Seltzer as Han, and rock singer Terri Nunn as Princess Leia?

Harrison Ford was hired for *Star Wars* on February 26, 1976 – exactly a month before principal shooting began. Old buddy Doug Rowe remembers, 'The day he got the part, he called me up and said "Come on over, and have some peanut butter and caviar!" '

Looking back, Lucas said he is glad that this trio worked out. He felt particularly at ease with

Ford, and allowed him a lot of space (no pun intended!) to develop the character of Han Solo, the cocky, buccaneer-style pilot of the Millennium Falcon. Lucas' first description of Solo, in his draft script of the movie, called him 'a James Dean-style star pilot, a cowboy in a starship: simple, sentimental and cocksure.' More than that, Ford would have to devise himself. It was a far cry from the roles Harrison was used to playing – roles where he had no say whatsoever.

'George Lucas gave me a lot of freedom to change little parts of dialogue which weren't comfortable,' Ford said. 'He knew the movie was based so strongly on the relationship among the three of us, that he encouraged our contributions.' As the straightforward actor once put it to his boss: 'You can type this shit, George, but you sure can't *say* it!'

Ford once told *Rock* magazine, 'I had a difficult time with lines like, "It'll take a megasecond for the nava computer to calculate the co-ordinates!" You feel silly, shooting guns that make no sound and destroying battleships that you're unable to see because the special effects won't be done for months.'

Although Ford was ecstatic about a starring role (the romantic lead, even) and was happy to be working with a prestigious director like Lucas, he did have his doubts about how *Star Wars* was going to be received by the public. Was the world really ready for a mega-budget space western? Would he become a laughing-stock in the industry? 'I really wasn't sure how that first film would do,' recalled Ford. 'I thought, either it would reach a wide audience who would recognize it as a fun, space-age western, or it would be so silly that my two kids would be embarrassed for me to even leave the house.'

Needless to say, audiences loved the rip-roaring, action-packed, good vs. evil story, a time-honoured genre spiffed up with three million dollars worth of fantastic special effects. All the elements were in place: the stoic sidekick (Chewbacca the Wookiee), the comic relief ('droids R2D2 and C3PO), the evil cattle baron . . .er, spacelord Darth Vader. *Star Wars* was not exactly *Star Trek*, boldly going where no man had gone before; rather, it boldly went exactly where thousands had gone before, and made it all seem new again. 'A magnificent film,' said *Daily Variety*. 'George Lucas set out to make the biggest possible adventure fantasy out of his memories of serials and older action epics, and he has succeeded brilliantly. . . . Harrison Ford is outstanding as a likeable mercenary pilot.' The *Los Angeles Times* called *Star Wars* 'a celebration . . . robust and free-wheeling.'

Han Solo was a future-day Errol Flynn, a swashbuckler the likes of whom we hadn't seen since *The Adventures of Robin Hood*. Soldier of fortune-cum-smuggler Han Solo had more of a past than ever translated to the screen – did you know Han was abandoned by space gypsies as an infant, raised by Wookiees until the age of twelve, and was a cadet at the Space Academy until he was chucked out for selling exam papers? To prepare for his role, Ford said he used to wear his costume under his clothes, and 'practise self-deprecating lines.'

Off to London went Harrison (he wasn't required for the early shots in Tunisia, luckily), to become unwittingly part of a new lease of life for the venerable EMI-Elstree Studio. Most of the movie was made without his help, though, back at LucasFilm's Industrial Light & Magic in Van Nuys, California (later rebuilt in San Rafael, early location of *American Graffiti*).

'I don't consider actors to be the first-line creative artists,' Ford once said. 'The directors and writers are the real poets of the system. I'm a craftsman.' That was never more true than in this film, where Ford, Hamill and Fisher spent most of their time emoting in front of blue chromatic screens, while Lucas dreamed up the action that would be taking place around them. It led to a certain amount of cabin fever in the halls of the Death Star, and claustrophobia begat outright giddiness at times. 'The only damper on the pure fun of that set,' recalled Ford, 'was the almost unanimous attitude of the English crew that we were totally out of our minds.'

Star Wars was a visual toy store. Not only did it become one of the biggest-grossing box office hits in history, but propelled the concept of movie merchandising to a new mega-buck level. Every kid had to have a copy of those nifty laser swords that Obi-Wan Kenobi and Vader fought with;

miniature Lukes and Leias sold like Ken and Barbie. If Kenner toys sold nothing but *Star Wars* items, the company would still be the fifth largest-grossing toy manufacturer in the world. Lucas-Films licensed *Star Wars* designer telephones, posters, lunchboxes, bicycles, pinball machines, and underwear. There was an official *Star Wars* fan-club ($5 membership) and a *Star Wars* video game that made $20 million for Parker Brothers. The soundtrack album made $16 million, and the novelization-of-the-movie paperback sold five million copies. *Star Wars* merchandising earned in excess of $1.5 *billion*. 'Personally, I had no emotional response to seeing Han Solo dolls,' was Harrison's predictable reaction to all this hoopla.

Star Wars was the first film ever to sell $10 million in tickets in one weekend; in its first year of distribution, the movie made more than $300 million. (Television rights alone were estimated at $60 million.) And since Lucas had offered his actors points – a percentage of the profits – as part of their salary, Ford and his two co-stars shared two per cent of that total. Two per cent may not sound like a huge piece of the pie, but when the pie is worth $300 million, it adds up to as much as $6 million. Naturally, the actors don't get that full amount off the top gross; net revenue per point has been estimated at $300,000 – plus ancillary rights, plus salaries, plus bonuses, plus plus. *Star Wars* didn't just make Harrison Ford famous. It made him very, very rich. Today, Ford's fortune has been estimated as in excess of $50 million, but he won't confirm that figure. In fact, his only comment on his fortune is: 'People would like to know exactly how rich I am, but it's none of their goddam business.'

Ford is well aware that Han Solo is not the most complex of characters. 'For Han, I keep my interpretation simple,' he said. 'If you put together all three of the characters in *Star Wars*, you'd have one whole personality.' Once, Harrison was asked what Han Solo thought of Harrison Ford. Putting himself back in character, he described his alter ego to *Omni* magazine: 'Harrison? He'd rather be an actor than star,' said 'Han.' 'I can handle that, though I wish he had working knowledge of science fiction. It was *torture* explaining the mechanical and space things to him.'

Ford later said, 'Han is no longer the only stamp in my passport, but somehow he has become part of me.' It was a lucky thing that Ford kept in touch with the Han Solo inside him, because he was going to need it. Lucas' vision of *Star Wars* wasn't merely to have it masquerade as part of a continuing serial; he actually planned for it to *be* one of an eventual nine-part saga. Had the expensive special effects of the first instalment proved to be an investor's nightmare, Lucas would have become known as a risk-taker who lost his bet. Instead, Lucas became known as a daring visionary who could do no wrong. *Star Wars* was nominated for ten Academy Awards, including Best Picture, Best Direction and Best Screenplay. It won four, for Art Direction, Costume Design, Score and

Special Effects – plus a special award for Sound Effects. The next episode of *Star Wars* would be no long shot; it would be a sure thing.

But all this special-effects wizardry takes years of preparation, and Harrison Ford had to do something to occupy himself until the inevitable *Star Wars II*. He debated: should he continue to take Han Solo-type roles, and rest on the laurels of his established success? Or should he try to find something more challenging, out of character with Solo? If he did the former, said Ford, 'I might make more money, but it wouldn't be long before I'd be bored and stereotyped.'

Of course, Harrison didn't have to decide overnight. He had enough money to retire, if he chose to, and certainly enough to take his time before rushing on to the next step. All this fortune and fame was rather a stunning turn of events, and a breather while he sorted out his new position in life – a position, he eventually decided, best left reasonably unchanged – was in order. He had his pick of parts, now. Amazing, he thought, that he went into this hoping only to earn enough money to qualify for health insurance!

'I guess I'd still be building furniture if I hadn't fallen in with George Lucas,' Ford once said with complete candour. 'I had been around for fifteen years, doing TV, doing small roles in features, until *Star Wars*. Now, a few of my problems have been solved, apparently forever – problems like how to pay the bills and like what will I do next, that kind of thing.'

Chapter Five

Keeping On

Carrie Fisher once said that Harrison Ford bears more than a passing resemblance to Han Solo. 'The role gets lost in Harrison,' she commented. 'I don't think there's a lot that's dissimilar between the character and the person. It's no accident that he plays a lot of heroes. He plays somebody you can rely on, who will take care of whatever it is – from a kid's hurt finger, to a murder, to saving the galaxy. He has that quality.'

Ford himself disagrees. 'I'm not at all like any of the heroes I play, except in my fantasies,' he said in 1984. 'I wish I could see only the heroics my characters perform on-screen but, unfortunately, I seem to be aware only of my mistakes.'

In the twenty months between the release of *Star Wars* and the first days of shooting its sequel,

Harrison Ford proceeded to grab every decent part he was offered . . . provided it in no way reminded him of Han Solo. He desperately wanted to avoid being pigeon-holed as a 'space cadet' for the rest of his professional life. 'It was critical that I have as many roles as possible between the first one (*Star Wars*) and the second (*Empire Strikes Back*),' he explained. 'I wanted to have a lot of characters on the other side.'

The next role Ford tackled was as the hillbilly Vietnam vet Kenny Boyd in the under-recognized movie *Heroes*, starring Henry Winkler (then typecast himself as the leather-jacketed Fonzie in the TV series *Happy Days*) and a pre-Oscar Sally Field. Ford played one of three war buddies whom Winkler – an escapee from the psych ward at a VA hospital – recruits in his quest to go West and start a worm farm.

Heroes was not a major commercial success although, with $20 million gross revenues and frequent television airplay, it wasn't a black mark on anyone's record by any means. The critics bestowed mixed reviews on the project, but those which mentioned Ford specifically were unvaryingly positive. The trade paper *Hollywood Reporter* wrote: 'Ford gives us an inkling of what this movie might have been. Behind his good old boy bravado, you feel the toll the war has taken on this man. When Ford is on-screen, the tiny echoes of old movies die away and *Heroes* takes on – briefly – the resonance of real life.'

From this critically respected, low-budget

sleeper, Ford next turned 180 degrees and accepted a part in the star-studded sequel to 1957's *The Guns of Navarone* – based on an Alistair MacLean novel and starring David Niven, Gregory Peck and Anthony Quinn – called *Force 10 From Navarone*. Ensemble cast war extravaganzas are seldom Academy Award fodder, but Ford was interested in both trying a new formula and working with the late Robert Shaw. Harrison became brash US Ranger Lt. Colonel Barnsby, in one of his most forgettable big-screen appearances.

The film was originally slated to shoot on location in Yugoslavia. But, due to bad weather conditions, the cast and crew spent their first weeks abroad trapped in their hotel rooms. The actors considered taking a brief detour to Italy while they waited for conditions to clear, but even that didn't work out: not only was it raining in Rome, but locals were being kidnapped and held for ransom at the rate of one a week. It was not a good place for a celebrity jaunt. Ford & Co. put on a stoic face, and waited for some Slavic sun.

Struggling under the weight of a deteriorating marriage (brought on in part by extended location shoots like this one), Ford went through the filming in bad humour. During the nine weeks on location in Yugoslavia, Ford said, 'the hardest thing we had to do on this film was get up in the morning.'

Trailers for *Force 10* hyped 'Harrison Ford, defending himself in a different kind of war.' The critics, however, were unimpressed. *Hollywood Reporter* commented that 'Ford hasn't gotten a fix on his character until the last 30 minutes.' *Newsweek* magazine said: 'Ford, required to look grim and determined throughout, hasn't decided if he's playing the story of GI Joe or Terry and the Pirates.' Perhaps the only notable fan of the film was President Jimmy Carter, who selected it as the Thanksgiving Day attraction at Camp David in 1979.

Soon after, a busy Ford flew off to London for *Hanover Street*, a sensitive, low-key love story also set during World War II. It was a project that had first been offered to Kris Kristofferson, and was ceded to Ford at the last minute (and at a far lower salary) when Kristofferson had to bow out. How did Harrison feel about being second choice? He turned down the part, of course.

'I did at first say no,' recalled Ford. 'I was still making *Force Ten From Navarone*, which was running a month over schedule, and I needed a break.' *Hanover* writer-director Peter Hyams grabbed a plane to the *Navarone* location, now on the island of Jersey, to try and change the actor's mind. 'We were night shooting a fight scene on top of a windy bluff overlooking the ocean,' recalled Ford. 'Peter and I talked all night in my trailer. I was impressed with his monomaniacal attitude.'

Ford became the dashing flyboy David Halloran, representing to war-weary British females a fantastic ideal of romance and freedom. His character ensnares (and later gallantly releases) Lesley-Anne Down, wife of an absent British intelligence officer. Interestingly, Ford's scenes with Down provided him with his first on-screen kiss – a remarkable achievement in movie virtue and abstinence, considering the number of films he had done to date. Compared to Harrison Ford, Shirley Temple was a pushover! 'I don't think that watching how the plumbing works is what people really want,' is Ford's estimation of sex in the cinema.

What Ford was trying to establish at this time – and what was becoming quite evident to the film community – was that he concerned himself with the quality of a role, and looked for versatility in his work. 'I don't choose films on the basis of whether I think they're going to be commercially successful,' Ford told *USA Today*. 'I'm recalling this bit of advice that Noel Coward gave to David Lean: "Do what pleases you and if people don't like it, get out of show business." I think that is probably the proper attitude.'

Hanover Street was not, unfortunately, a crowd-pleaser. Although some praised Ford's downbeat portrayal of his war-hero character, others found the material simply too hackneyed. Charles Champlin of the *Los Angeles Times* was impressed with the actor's developing range, saying 'Ford, who excelled as a dazed Vietnam veteran in *Heroes*, gives the pilot a kind of glum, almost sour, intensity.' But Vincent Canby in the *New York Times* wrote, 'I've no idea whether the film will do anything for Mr Ford's screen popularity. He's more a comic strip character here than he was in *Star Wars*, which was a live action cartoon.'

Typecasting would have been comfortable for 'Han Solo,' but it would neither prove Harrison's acting flexibility nor challenge him to new plateaus in his craft. Some of his choices may have been ill-advised, but Ford was looking first for an interesting movie, and second for a juicy part. Unlike most bankable actors, he was uninterested in star vehicles – flat films that would surround him with mediocrity, and make him look that much better by comparison. He would rather be one stone of the Crown Jewels than an eye-catching pendant.

'I want to be in *movies* that are the star,' he said, in his self-effacing way. 'I think I've been as lucky as anyone can be.'

Frantically flying from place to place, script to script, Ford took a cameo part in old friend Francis Ford Coppola's controversial blockbuster, *Apocalypse Now*. Ford was almost unrecognized as 'The Colonel.' He was listed in the credits without a proper name but was jokingly called 'Colonel G. Lucas' by Ford himself – the title used by Coppola in a close-up of Ford's uniform nametag. 'When George Lucas saw *Apocalypse* he didn't even recognize me!' laughed Harrison. (An aside for trivia fans: Martin Sheen's lead role was as Capt. Benjamin Willard, which combines both of Harrison's progeny into one name.)

He also made an uncredited appearance,

reprising the role of Bob Falfa (now a motorcycle cop, *Officer* Falfa, with a particular dislike of dope-smoking hippies), for *More American Graffiti*, which was filmed under the working title *Purple Haze*. Although largely unnoticed by the world in general, *More American Graffiti* was actually a fairly advanced piece of film-making, utilizing split-screen effects and multiple story-lines to advance the life stories of the original cast members. But since most of the *Graffiti I* alumni didn't come back for seconds, the concept fell short. Will Seltzer, the young actor aced out by Ford for the part of Han Solo, got to play the younger brother of the absent Richard Dreyfuss. *Variety* called *More American Graffiti* 'one of the most innovative and ambitious films of the last five years, but by no means is it one of the most successful.'

The roles were interesting, but Ford wanted a change of pace as well, and decided to try his hand at comedy. After all, his dry wit and sarcasm were a lot of what made the Han Solo character come to life.

In *The Frisco Kid*, Ford plays another soft-hearted cynic, Tommy Lillard, a professional out-law who takes under his wing an innocent Polish rabbi (Gene Wilder), lost in the wild west of 1850 and searching for San Francisco. Lillard, purporting to be nothing less than a bank robber, card shark and womanizer rolled into one, develops an uncharacteristic attachment for the rabbi, and the pair's journey takes some bizarre and amusing twists.

'The two pivotal characters,' wrote the *Motion Picture Product Digest*, 'are played by Gene Wilder and Harrison Ford with an amiability and zest that are hard to resist.' While the ever-unfriendly Vincent Canby called Ford 'little more than a stalwart straight man' and felt the film was a case of 'the wrong talent for the wrong material,' the trade magazine *Variety* had kinder words for the effort: 'Excellent counterpoint is provided by Ford, who finally lives up to the potential he displayed in *Star Wars*. As a cowboy who reluctantly adopts the greenhorn for their westward journey, Ford provides the perfect foil for Wilder's gaffes, and their scenes play wonderfully.'

If Ford's choice of roles seems to have no rhyme or reason, they do have one common thread: each was blessed by Ford's son Ben, who was then 12 years old. Harrison always sought the advice and approval of his eldest before taking an assignment – sort of an informal demographic survey. It was Ben who first predicted the success of *Star Wars*, long before the box offices opened to land office business. And, after a visit to the location of *Frisco Kid* during his Thanksgiving vacation, Ben pronounced his father's newest venture a hit. 'Gene Wilder's really funny, Dad,' declared Ben, and he likened his father to one of Ford's own all-time favourite straight men – Bud Abbott.

Amazingly, there were five films in all in the period – less than two years, remember – between *Star Wars* and pre-production of *The*

Empire Strikes Back. Quite a full plate, even for someone whose main goal in life was to have enough work. 'One of the greatest pleasures of my life is working,' said Ford. Only a month after completing *The Frisco Kid* in the late winter of 1979, it was time to fly to Norway to take up the further adventures of Han Solo. But, as it turned out, Ford had a few adventures of his own before uttering the first lines of his next script.

Chapter Six

Box Office Hero

Production on *The Empire Strikes Back* was scheduled to start on March 5, 1979. The first piece of film due to be put in the can was set on the ice planet Hoth, the location of the galactic rebels' new home base station. A Norwegian glacier near the city of Finse, six thousand feet above sea level, impersonated the ice planet – almost too realistically. Nature put on a production of her own, one that made the behind-the-scenes machinations for shooting *Empire* almost an action-adventure movie in and of themselves.

Hurling ice and snow out of the Arctic Circle, Mother Nature blitzed northern Europe with one of the harshest winters in recorded history. Finse – population 75, average temperature that month ten degrees below zero – was isolated by blizzards and avalanches. The railway link to Oslo, the only transport in or out of the remote mountain pass location, was totally obscured.

While the production crew waited for Harrison's arrival on the set to film a scene where Han rescues Luke Skywalker, Harrison waited for rescue himself. The train taking him to Finse was trapped in a tunnel that had collapsed under the weight of the snow; Ford was, literally, on ice.

Frantic, the location managers chartered a special train equipped with massive snow-ploughs, and sent it out to hunt for their star. In true Tinseltown tradition, the snowbreaker train forged a path through drifts fifty feet high to Geilo, a ski resort thirty miles east of Finse. Production crew members, keeping in contact with railway authorities by radio, heard the drama's finale with relief. Ford was unloaded from the train on a giant shovel, and made it to the set safely at midnight.

Having starred in his own real-life drama – with neither stuntmen, script nor soundtrack – Ford was on the set the next morning, shooting the picture's opening scene with Mark Hamill. It must have been a bit anti-climactic. As Ford said later: 'Part of professionalism is showing up on time and knowing your lines. But I have never before learned them in an avalanche, or reached a set in a snow plough!'

The monumental interiors for *The Empire Strikes Back* were again filmed at the EMI-Elstree Studios, where a huge stage – called the Star Wars

Stage, naturally – was built specifically for the production of *Empire*. At two hundred and fifty feet long, one hundred and twenty-two feet wide and forty-five feet high, the set could handle the largest props – like the full-scale Millennium Falcon, weighing in at forty tons and divided into sixteen separate sections for mobility. The Falcon was constructed in the Welsh hangar where the giant Sunderland flying boats of the Thirties had been built, and was carried across Great Britain by a convoy of trucks to its final destination outside London. Once the Falcon arrived, things on the EMI-Elstree set were rather cramped – especially as most of Stage Three had burned down while Stanley Kubrick was filming *The Shining*.

The other half of the production duo for *Empire* was the Industrial Light and Magic facility in Marin County, California. That's where George Lucas and producer Gary Kurtz oversaw the design and construction of the special *Star Wars* cameras, with visual effects specialists Brian Johnson and Richard Edlund, and where the interaction between live and F/X was correlated by editor Paul Hirsch.

Except for the absence of Alec Guinness, who was recovering from eye surgery, the first days of shooting *Empire* were home territory for the now-familiar cast. Each had returned to the set a veteran of other productions: Ford had a healthy portfolio under his belt, from the five very different parts he had undertaken over the past two years. Mark Hamill had completed *Corvette*

Summer and *The Big Red One*. Carrie Fisher, besides studying at Sarah Lawrence College, had performed in the made-for-TV movie *Come Back Little Sheba*, and in *Leave Yesterday Behind*.

Newcomers to the cast included smooth and sexy Billy Dee Williams as Lando Calrissian, and Yoda, the Jedi master, played by a Frank Oz Muppet.

At the last moment, the reunion was completed when Alec Guinness confirmed that he would be able to return. But Ford's reappearance was not assured, as it turned out. Of all the starring players, only Harrison had not agreed to appear in future *Star Wars* sequels when he first signed his contract. He re-negotiated his deal, and initially asked for a huge increase in salary. That was a bluff, however, and George Lucas knew it. What Ford really wanted – and got – was the assurance that his character would become a more rounded human being in *The Empire Strikes Back*, a deeper and more three-dimensional role for Ford to tackle. His final salary was identical to that of Hamill and Fisher.

The human relationships that barely began to be established in *Star Wars* – between Han and Luke, Han and Princess Leia, and Leia and Luke – were given a little space to grow in *Empire*. As always, Ford's personal input had a great deal to do with his character development. The plot-line followed the rebels after they achieve destruction of the *Star Wars* Death Star: Darth Vader, who escaped death in episode one, sends out probes to locate his enemies. The sub-plot, dealing with Luke's realization that Vader is his father, gives *Empire* an identity of its own: a downbeat cliff-hanger that goes against the old Hollywood tradition of good guys in white hats ending every film with another notch in the belt for Truth and Justice and their horses intact. *Empire* ends with hero Han being put into carbonite freeze – and, as he is lowered into the dreadful decoction, his parting shot is provided by a suggestion from actor Ford. 'I love you!' yells Princess Leia to her disappearing devotee. 'I know!' Solo cheekily replies.

Carrie Fisher described the relationship of Han and Leia as 'like in the Thirties films, with Fred and Ginger fighting up to the last reel. It's Bogart and Bacall, Tracy and Hepburn. It's two independent people, quarrelling and fighting – and then they neck. That's what it is – romance on celluloid. Seriously, I believe both characters are more fully dimensional in *Empire Strikes Back* than in *Star Wars*. In the first film, the action was so intense that it gave us no time to think about one another. Now, George Lucas has given the Princess a more full-blooded feel about her – and the role was much more challenging to play.'

Ford, who says of Solo that 'I intentionally keep my interpretation simple,' had hoped his swashbuckler would not merely be freeze-dried at the end of *Empire*. He suggested to Lucas that the character be killed off. He was, he said, a little burned-out on this egocentric persona. 'George,' deadpanned Ford, 'didn't agree.'

The chemistry between the lead actors wasn't the only thing that worked for *The Empire Strikes Back*. As always, the toys stole the show. At the Fifty-Third Annual Academy Awards, *Empire* won a Special Achievement Award for Visual Effects, as well as an Oscar for Technical Achievement in Sound, one for Original Score (by John Williams) and a nomination for Best Art Direction. The film, whose initial budget estimate of $18.5 million had grown to $22 million ($33 million, if you count bank interest) earned $300 million in initial release. The day before the film opened, a special telephone information hot-line literally burned out local phone circuits when 130,000 calls came in at once.

'*The Empire Strikes Back* is a worthy sequel to *Star Wars*,' wrote *Variety*, 'equal in both technical mastery and characterizations. The only box-office question is how many earthly trucks it will take to carry the cash to the bank.' 'I especially liked [the] handling of Han Solo in this outing,' opined Arthur Knight in the *Hollywood Reporter*. 'Han not only grows in stature, but his romantic passages with Princess Leia seem more urgent and heartfelt than in the earlier chapter.'

So, after a success like that one, what do you do for an encore? If you're George Lucas, you give 'em another chorus of what worked the first time around. Change the lyrics, switch the setting – and bring in a creative dynamo named Steven Spielberg to contribute his two cents (give or take ten million) to the project.

Three names were magic in the entertainment industry in the late Seventies: George Lucas, Steven Spielberg and Francis Ford Coppola. In 1978, the topmost of the top-grossing films in history to date were Lucas' *Star Wars*, Spielberg's *Jaws*, and Coppola's *The Godfather*. These were the men with the Midas touch, *auteurs* who could do no wrong. In 1986, Lucas and Coppola would make headlines when they united to create the 3-D spectacular (and, per minute, the most expensive motion picture ever) *Captain Eo*. In 1980, the news was that Lucas and Spielberg were getting together – professionally, for the first time in their eleven-year friendship – to create *Raiders of the Lost Ark*.

Harrison Ford began his career with Lucas and Coppola. Now, he was about to add Spielberg to his list. Before the first scenes of *Raiders* were shot, exhibitors were bidding for the right to show this guaranteed blockbuster, a thrill-a-minute Saturday-morning serial concept piece set in an exotic time and place.

George Lucas said he first came up with the idea for *Raiders* himself. In fact, 'Indiana' was the name of his wife Marcia's pet Alaskan malamute. 'The whole project started about ten years ago,' he recalled in 1981, 'when I had an idea to do an action-adventure kind of serial film. It was actually about the same time I came up with the idea for *Star Wars*. But I got more interested in *Star Wars*, so I put this one on the shelf, and figured I'd do it some day.'

Years later, he and Steven Spielberg happened to be vacationing in Hawaii at the same time, and they discussed the possibility that Lucas had kept on the back burner for so long. This time, January 1979, they put the idea front and centre, and work began.

George Lucas had in mind Tom Selleck, TV's 'Magnum P.I.', for the role of Indiana Jones, saying the part needed a 'jock jester' to lighten its tone. CBS television, though, had no intention of releasing Selleck from his contractual commitment to them. It was Spielberg who opted for Harrison Ford to star in this epic – on the basis of having seen him work for Lucas. 'It was getting to the end of the time for choosing a lead,' remembered Spielberg, 'and I had gone to see *The Empire Strikes Back*. Harrison was so obviously right for Indiana Jones that George and I approached him the next day.' Hoardings across the nation testified to the fact that Ford said yes, although his first reaction was to play hard-to-get. When informed that he was being sought for the part of Indy, Ford – who knew he was second choice after Selleck – told Dale Pollock, 'They could find me if they wanted me.'

Ford said that as soon as he was actually offered the job, he recognized 'a really good part in what could be a really good movie.' But he also shared the same concern that Spielberg and Lucas did: that this character and this film must be distinct from that other character in that other thrill-a-minute Saturday-morning serial type thing, called *Star Wars*.

'I think there's a similarity between Solo and Jones,' said Ford, 'but they're as unlike each other as they are alike. They're both fast-talking, smooth guys, in a certain way. But Han Solo is less complicated than Indiana, a less sophisticated person. Jones is a character who has some other dimensions. He's kind of a swashbuckling hero type, but he has human frailties, fears and money problems, and therefore is more down to earth. He does brave things, but I wouldn't describe him as a hero. He teaches, but I wouldn't describe him as an intellectual.'

Still, Ford did not ignore the cerebral aspects of his character, and studied for the part by reading every archaeology book dating from the 1930s that he could find.

Since *Raiders of the Lost Ark* was set in 1936, Indiana Jones had to be more capable than Han Solo: he couldn't rely on futuristic gadgetry to keep him at arm's distance from his enemies. All Jones had was his wit, a battered trilby and a bullwhip (okay, and a pistol) to hold the world at bay.

That hat, by the way, turned out to be one of the trickier bits of Ford's work as Jones. Doing his own stunts as often as not, Ford said the toughest thing he had to learn was how to run, jump and fight – and never lose the darn hat. 'Actually,' he joked, 'it's kept on with little carpet tacks. No, really, they use double-sided tape to keep the hat from falling off. A little trick of the trade.'

Spielberg envisioned Ford's Indy as an archetypal hero, a new version of that time-honoured literary construct, The Resourceful Man. The director commented during production that 'Harrison is a very original leading man. In this film, he is a remarkable combination of Errol Flynn in *The Adventures of Don Juan* and Humphrey Bogart as Fred C. Dobbs in *Treasure of the Sierra Madre*. He can be villainous and romantic all at once. He carries this movie wonderfully.'

Ford saw Indy as inspired by the classic pulp magazine heroes, like Doc Savage or G–8 and his Battle Aces. Unlike Han Solo, Jones is not merely one part of a strong ensemble cast; Ford alone had a great deal of leeway to develop his character, and more responsibility for the final look and feel of the picture.

Talking to *Omni* magazine, Ford called his new creation 'really quite different from the other characters I've played. He's a scholary man, a professor of archaeology and an expert on the occult. Otherwise, he's just an average guy who finds himself in swashbuckling circumstances, and rises to the occasion.'

There are parallels between Ford and Jones: in many ways, Ford is also an ordinary guy who found himself in extraordinary circumstances. Almost overnight, he went from dependable sideman to powerful superstar. But, rather than use his newfound influence to demand fancier dressing rooms and longer limousines, Ford wielded his clout to exert control over his own destiny – to mould his part, to have meaningful input into the final product.

Above: With Carrie
Fisher and Mark
Hamill, promoting
Star Wars

Left: A friendly pat
on the cheek at the
LA International
Film Expo

Above (with sons Ben and Willard) and *left:* *Raiders of the Lost Ark* showing, Deauville Film Festival

Right: Raiders of the Lost Ark

Above: Holidaying in Bora Bora

Right: With wife, Melissa, at a showing of *Blade Runner*

Far right: *Blade Runner*

Left: Melissa, awarded best drama writer

Below: Blade Runner

Right: Melissa and Harrison in Los Angeles

Over: Promoting *Witness* at the Cannes Film Festival

Ford's goal, as always, was a better movie, not a higher profile. The play's the thing, to coin a phrase. 'It's not a question of privilege,' said Ford about demanding creative control. 'It's a question of responsibility, to define the character for the audience, to make the film as good as you can.'

For *Raiders*, Ford collaborated on Indy's costumes, helped choreograph fight sequences – anything to make Jones a more believable character. Nor did all that detail come easy. Indiana Jones is an expert with a bullwhip; unsurprisingly, real-life Ford isn't. He had to learn – the hard way. Stunt co-ordinator Glenn Randall recalled: 'I was whip specialist, but Harrison had no experience with a whip. We spent hours and hours learning it. There were many times that Harrison accidentally hit himself, but he just bit his lip and kept practising.'

Ford decided not to use his hard-won whip expertise in one memorable scene from *Raiders*, a scene where once again it was Ford's intuition that led to an important bit of cinematic business. Most fans are well aware that, in the famous take where Jones shoots down the big bad guy who is facing him off with a broadsword, Indy was originally supposed to duel the man with his whip. That resigned sigh that Indy heaves as he rolls his eyes and pulls his pistol is the catalyst for one of the best audience reactions in the movie.

Ford recalled the chain of events that led to changing this particular segment of screenplay: 'I was in my fifth week of dysentery at the time. The location was an hour and a half drive from where we stayed. I'm riding to the set at 5.30 am, and I can't wait to storm up to Steven with this idea. I'd worked out that we could save four whole days on this lousy location with the change. Besides which, I think it was right and important, because what's more vital in the character's mind is finding Marion. He doesn't have time for another fight. But, as is very often the case, when I suggested this to Steven – "Let's just shoot the sucker" – he said, "I just thought of the same thing this morning." '

This empathy between the director and the star explains why, while most stars have to fight for creative involvement, director Spielberg encouraged Ford's input. He said he respected Harrison as a person of insight and intelligence, as well as an exceptional actor.

'Harrison Ford was more than just an actor playing a role in *Raiders of the Lost Ark*,' noted Spielberg. 'He was involved in a lot of decision-making about the movie as we went along. And this wasn't by contract; it was because I sensed an exceptionally strong mind and a very smart person, and called on him time and time again.'

While *Raiders* stuck firmly to the action-adventure formula that had worked so well in Ford's prior blockbusters, his increased range in this role was not lost on observers. 'I had not thought that Ford had it in him to convey such a marvellously weary doggedness of spirit as he confronts the inexhaustible wiles of the world's villains,' said the *Village Voice*. Noted *Variety*, 'Ford marks a major turning point in his career as the occasionally frail but ever invincible mercenary-archaeologist, projecting a riveting strength of character throughout.'

Raiders of the Lost Ark cost more than $20 million to make (up from an original estimate of $7 million), and some of the money went in strange and unusual places. Production began in April, 1983 in La Rochelle, one hundred miles north of Bordeaux in France's prime wine country. Six thousand live reptiles – including pythons, cobras and boa constrictors – along with a snake expert and his five assistants, were transported onto the set. The cobras measured six to twelve feet in length, and every crew member had to be alerted that the creatures were as dangerous as they looked. Each staffer was warned to wear protective clothing, high rubber boots and strengthened canvas trousers and jackets.

Explains snake expert Mike Culling, 'The cobras can kill inside three minutes, and can paralyze a person in thirty seconds. Their double fangs can punch through thick leather, and deliver sufficient venon to stun their victim or make him unconscious.'

With these lethal 'extras' on the set, special precautions were taken. 'We couldn't film these scenes without having serum standing by, with a doctor to administer it,' said Culling. 'In fact, the day before we started shooting, we discovered that the serum we had was out of date, and we had to have replacement stock flown in from Paris – the only place we could find it.'

Also in the 'cast' were fifty live tarantulas, which Spielberg personally affixed to the clothing of actors Ford and Alfred Molina. Thirty-six live beetles were insured as 'props' by the Fireman's Fund. But then, what's a little entomological extravagance when your movie grosses more than $231 million in its first year ($335 million to date, worldwide), pushing it up to Number Four on the list of All-Time Highest Grossing Films?

Worthy of special mention in the crew of *Raiders of the Lost Ark* – and soon to establish a long-term relationship with Harrison Ford – was his stuntman. Although Ford does many of his own feats of derring-do (he says the easy ones are often the most dangerous, because you *prepare* for the tough ones), *Raiders* introduced him to the man who would double for him in his next three film efforts: Englishman Vic Armstrong. Not only did Armstrong have 19 years experience as a stuntman – in such films as *Never Say Never*, *Superman* and *Dune*, to name only three out of a total of 200 – but the resemblance between the two men is uncanny.

Ford first met Armstrong, four years his junior, on location in Tunisia. He couldn't help but strike up an acquaintance with the man – after all, if they were wearing the same outfit, hardly anyone could even tell them apart. They're the same height, weight, colouring, they even switched clothes on purpose at times, to give their teammates a laugh. Ford said that Armstrong is worth his weight in gold – not to mention the $200,000 a year the man makes from his job. It's enough to buy Vic his lovely farm near Pinewood Studios in Windsor, where he lives quietly between pictures, though Armstrong said it didn't take much more than a whistle to coax him onto the cast list for the next Indiana Jones movie . . . or the next one after that. (Indy III is currently scheduled to begin filming in early '87, if Steven Spielberg has finished his *Peter Pan* project by then.)

Third Indiana Jones or no third Indiana Jones, though, Harrison Ford was elevated to full-blown superstardom by *Raiders of the Lost Ark*. He was no single leg of a triangle in this movie; he was The Hero. And he was perhaps the only actor alive who could boast – after the receipts on *Raiders* were counted – of having earned for his bosses more than one *billion* dollars on-screen.

Chapter Seven

Get Serious

The topsy-turvy world of motion pictures sometimes sounds like a Rodney Dangerfield comedy
routine: the folks who are the most successful are
the same ones who don't get no respect. Accord-
ing to the average professional film critic, a movie
that appeals to the mass audience can't possibly
be any good on an artistic level: this would be a
contradiction in terms. When's the last time
Judith Krantz won the Pulitzer Prize, after all?

Harrison Ford, to whom quality was always
more important than stardom (if not quantity),
found himself in an ironic position in the 1980s.
He was a mega-star who got no critical acclaim for
the excellence of his work. (*Variety* and the
Hollywood Reporter were notable exceptions to this
rule, as trade magazines are perfectly willing to
include the bottom line in their critical equa-

tions.) The man who wanted to be an actor rather than a celebrity suddenly found himself a celebrity whom few considered a serious actor. He met the problem with his typical tenacity, and began searching for deeper, more meaningful roles.

Oddly enough, the part that first proved to film critics that there was more to Ford than wisecracks, stunt work and good F/X was, thematically, almost a combination of everything he had done before. The Ridley Scott movie *Blade Runner*, based on the late sci-fi great Philip K. Dick's novelette *Do Androids Dream of Electric Sheep?*, cast Ford as detective Rick Deckard – again living in the future, again challenged by improbable circumstance, and again infused with a Thirties' pulp-novel sensibility. This time, Ford played the stereotypical hard-boiled cop, forced out of retirement in a year–2019 megatropolis to hunt down dangerous 'replicants' – genetically engineered beings all but indistinguishable from humans.

Ford described *Blade Runner* as 'an old tale with new twists and wrinkles. It's a story that could have been written by Raymond Chandler,' he said. Fittingly, the movie was shot on the same Warner Brothers' backlot streets that Humphrey Bogart stalked in *film noir* classics like *The Maltese Falcon* and Chandler's own *The Big Sleep*. This time, though, the 'tec's arsenal included flying police cars and voice-operated computers that could all but read minds.

Director Scott described Ford's character as 'still very human, despite all the gadgetry. With all this high technology and sophisticated gear, Deckard is fallible. He's quite Marlowesque – a man who follows a hunch to the end.'

Ford called the spike-haired Deckard a 'reluctant detective, who dreams like a middle-aged Elvis Costello. He's a skilled investigator, an expert in his field, but he's a little out of practice when the story opens. He's lost his motor drive. Exterminating people, even non-human ones, is not something he likes to do, and he's not comfortable with it. He's very tough, but he's no match for a top-of-the-line replicant.'

Even when Han Solo was turned into a wall plaque at the end of *The Empire Strikes Back*, you never got the feeling that Harrison Ford's was a persona who could *lose*. Rick Deckard is a man who has come to grips with the possibility of failure. The complex sleuth is 'a man of two minds about everything,' as Ford saw him. His obsessions and his ambiguity made Deckard a fascinating challenge for the actor.

'It's totally unlike anything I've ever done before,' Ford said. '*Star Wars* and *Empire* were science fiction, but they were space fantasies. *Blade Runner* is a traditional big-city detective story, transplanted into a science fiction environment. It's real and gritty.' It was also a chance for Ford to step out of the charmed Lucas–Spielberg–Coppola circle, and prove that he was perfectly capable of working with new directors and producers.

Ridley Scott had handled the concept of 'skewed tradition' brilliantly once before. His hit *Alien* was basically a standard haunted house chiller, set in a sci-fi arena. Well known for careful use of set design and sound effects, Scott turned *Blade Runner* into a classy piece of film-making.

'The story has an element of psychological drama I've never dealt with before in a film, and it takes place in a world no one has even seen,' said Ford, adding, 'I have no desire to have films written for me or to produce my own projects. I prefer to find something that already has a life of its own, to which I can then add my contribution. That way, we can go further.'

Ford's willingness to 'go further' extends to the physical appearance of his characters. While he may not put on fifty pounds like Robert De Niro did for *Raging Bull*, or pull his eye-teeth like ambitious young Nicolas Cage did for *Birdy*, Ford does mould his characters through their clothing, hairstyles and mannerisms. It was his suggestion that Bob Falfa wear that trademark straw cowboy hat, way back when, and it was a particular hat – a Sam Spade-like, shop-worn fedora – he envisioned for Rick Deckard, too. Unfortunately, Indiana Jones already used that prop the previous season. So, in order to make Deckard look 'like nobody you've ever seen,' Ford told the hairdresser to 'shave it off.' Until the punkish final version of the Deckard hair grew in, cohorts on the set were calling Harrison 'Daddy Warbucks.'

Blade Runner, like *American Graffiti*, was a film whose alumni went on to bigger and better things. Daryl Hannah made her first big-screen appearance as the doomed (and startlingly athletic) replicant, Pris, long before she hit with *Splash* (directed by *Graffiti* alumnus Ron Howard, ironically) and *Legal Eagles*. Rutger Hauer, before playing heroic in *Ladyhawke* and demonic in *The Hitcher*, played messianic in *Blade Runner*, ending the film on a symbolic note as he died, crucifixion-style, literally with a nail through his palm.

Blade Runner is now considered a classic, but at the time of its release it earned mixed reviews. Dark-hued visions of a violent future, layered with religious allegory, are not the fluff of which sequels are made. Phrases like 'too arty, too avant-garde' and 'too stylish for today's audiences' reflected the general opinion. 'Philip Marlowe meets Frankenstein,' *Playboy* called it. The *Hollywood Reporter*, however, was not blind to Ford's input. 'Ford . . . is perfectly cast as the scruffy hunter, a character he endows with enough personality and vulnerability to create all the necessary audience identification and caring.' *Blade Runner* was particularly taken to task by the *New York Times* for its graphic violence – a harbinger of the *Temple of Doom* brouhaha to come – but is, nonetheless, a consistently popular feature in film class and at art and revival houses.

The film grossed $29 million domestically, significantly less than it cost to make, distribute and promote. Yet, *Blade Runner* gave Harrison Ford an invaluable new character dimension and brought him a fresh segment of the movie-going audience: the 'serious' fan. It also gave him the opportunity to do something that, for a romantic hero, he does rather seldom on-screen: fall in love . . . even if it was with an android.

There was hardly a break for Harrison between the downbeat sci-fi of *Blade Runner* and its upbeat obverse in *Return of the Jedi* (originally *Revenge of the Jedi*, and changed when Lucas decided that Jedi knights shouldn't be vengeful). Principal photography for the third *Star Wars* instalment began in January, 1982 for a projected release date of May 25, 1983 – the sixth anniversary of the release of the original *Star Wars*.

Director Richard Marquand spent twelve weeks shooting at the now-legendary EMI-Elstree Studio, and another eight weeks out on location. Special effects, of course, were once again done at Lucas' ILM – and took almost a year on their own.

By the time the lead trio of actors returned, each had racked up another load of individual credits. Mark Hamill had done the Broadway play, *The Elephant Man*, and played Mozart in the national touring company of Peter Shaffer's *Amadeus*. Carrie Fisher had done the film *Under the Rainbow*, and appeared in the award-winning Broadway drama, *Agnes of God*. Harrison Ford had taken up semi-permanent resident at movie houses worldwide as Indiana Jones.

Jedi took over all nine sound stages of EMI, filling every available space with creature workshops (you didn't think the musical trio of Max Rebo, Sy Snootles and Droopy McCool *auditioned*, did you?), prop-making facilities and elaborate wardrobe stations. The scale of the production is exemplified by the sheer vastness of the sets: Stage Six alone has a million and a half cubic feet capacity. Three different sets were constructed inside the giant room, including Jabba the Hutt's desert palace and the Imperial Death Star docking bay. A new Imperial Shuttle was built to full scale – the undercarriage alone weighed five tons – and positioned in the docking bay. The full-size Millennium Falcon was taken out of the warehouse and reassembled, as was Luke Skywalker's X-wing fighter.

Although no one doubted certain commercial success for *Jedi*, there was by now a growing sense of déjà vu among the players. They were going through the motions, in many ways, although no one can deny that they gave it the old school try. Ford, who had already asked to be killed off rather than go through another turn at Han Solo, softened his input to the movie. The lack of personal contribution was apparent to his old friends at *Variety*, whose industry review noted: 'Harrison Ford, who was such an essential element of the first two outings, is present more in body than in spirit this time, given little to do but react to special effects.'

To recount briefly the events of the so-far final

chapter in the saga of Luke, Leia and what's-his-name, *Return of the Jedi* pits Commander Skywalker and Princess Organa against the toad-like crime-lord Jabba to rescue a carbonited Solo from the desert planet Tatooine. Next, it's off to the forest planet of the furry Ewoks (merchandised to the hilt, and later spun off for television) for the sabotage of an Imperial station and simultaneously out into space for a battle royal between the Rebel Armada and the Empire's newest model of the Death Star. While these laser-bright action scenes kept audiences on the edges of their seats, it's important to remember that the film was made in layers – all the shiny bits added at Industrial Light and Magic – and the most exciting pieces on-screen were often the most boring to actually make.

Take the thrilling air motorcycle race, one of the fastest-moving scenes in *Jedi*. The crew went to a stand of giant redwoods near Crescent City, California and employed some 200 local citizens as extras – not to mention a full-time landscaping staff to keep the forest floor looking untrampled. For the stars, the whole episode was considerably less than thrilling.

'It might be the most exciting part of the film, but it was the most boring *to* film,' said Carrie Fisher. She explained that while viewers saw Luke and Leia racing past and darting around pines at breakneck pace, wind rushing through their costumes, what was happening in the studio was less impressive. Hamill and Fisher sat on dummy sky-cycles in front of a blank blue screen, while the director shouted out appropriate reactions to what would be happening to them in the finished product: ' "Now you're coming near a tree . . . bank to the left . . . veer to the right . . . look over your shoulder, that's it" . . . what a relief when it was over,' said Fisher. Then, all the bits were sewn together and, thanks to Lucas and producer Howard Kazanjian, the seams never show.

Return of the Jedi saw Han Solo back in business – and Harrison Ford moving to the top of his. In 1983, the Marketing Evaluations research firm surveyed the public, and discovered that Harrison Ford ranked third overall in popularity, right behind Eddie Murphy and Alan Alda, and right ahead of Bill Murray and Clint Eastwood. (Fickle, aren't we?) Ford was closer to megastar status than ever, but still a good way from the serious critical acclaim he desired. One more movie, *Indiana Jones and the Temple of Doom*, was yet to come before the role that would give him acting accolades and an Oscar nomination.

Temple of Doom pits Indy against a loathsome adversary in a desperate quest for a magical stone. Jones, his sidekick Short Round (played by Ke Huy Quan) and nightclub singer Willie Scott (played by Kate Capshaw) are thrown together by fate and tossed in a stuntwork salad of hair-raising event after cliff-hanging escape.

Doom had a $27.5 million production budget, and was shot on location in Sri Lanka, Macao and

England. Not just the crew travelled from the Orient to the UK: the handlers responsible for the movie's two pythons booked the snakes into their own hotel room, under the names 'Mr and Mrs Longfellow.' This couple wasn't exploited for terror, however; this time, Steven Spielberg reached into his memory for yet another primal, childhood fear, and littered the set with a collection of creepy-crawly insects that would make a mummy cringe.

This film was Saturday morning action done to a high lustre. Some of the stunts had never been attempted before on-screen – and some may never be duplicated, unless Lucas and Spielberg do it themselves. One particularly breathtaking sequence has Indy falling from a tall building through a series of canopies, without the camera ever seeming to cut away. Stuntman Vic Armstrong, who doubled for Ford in the long tracking shot, allows that a special rig was used to break his fall, but to this day won't reveal the details. In another tricky sequence, Indy is trapped on a rickety old bridge over a yawning chasm – but, in this case, the double was no double, and the gorge was really 300 feet down.

'We were lucky enough to find an accessible gorge right nearby, a construction site where a British company was building a large dam,' said *Doom* producer Frank Marshall. 'There, we had top-notch engineers and workers with convenient equipment to string the bridge with steel and cable. Once the bridge was up, we dressed it to look old and rickety.' The bodies that the audience sees falling from the bridge after Indy cuts the ropes are really air-powered dummies. Valves to their limbs make them kick and flail pneumatically as they fall.

Although Armstrong took over for the really dicey stunts, Harrison himself performed a great number of them. 'There are so many opportunities for characterization in physical action,' Harrison said. 'Really, that *is* the character – in these moments of action, you see Indiana Jones most clearly.'

The toughest one for Ford would have seemed to be one of the simplest: riding on elephant-back. 'Riding an elephant is *very* uncomfortable,' frowned Ford. 'I developed an antipathy towards elephant riding. You ride with your legs in a hyper-extended position to accommodate the girth of the animal right over its shoulders. First one leg then the other is pulled forward, which tends to spread you apart – like being stretched on a medieval rack, I imagine. I'm not surprised that mahouts generally walk next to their animals!'

It's natural that Ford developed a strong disinclination towards elephant riding, because that's how he managed to rupture an already stressed spinal disc during filming. Although he specifically attributes the condition to one particular leap performed about a third of the way into the production, he said, 'I think it was the elephants that really did me in.'

Ford's injury was not terribly serious for him, but it was almost fatal to the production. He had to be flown back to Los Angeles for emergency surgery, and was out of commission for six weeks. A friend, Howard Becker, remembers visiting Harrison in his hospital room. 'After the operation, he used a relatively tenacious and disciplined rehabilitation – stretching, a type of yoga if you will. He was working his muscles very hard. I was worried – I kept telling him to slow down. As a former athlete – I had a track scholarship at college – I know that strong people can sometimes come back too fast. But he healed completely, and did it faster than the doctors expected. He's a very strong-willed person.'

In the end, happily, Ford recovered full mobility, and returned to complete the shoot. In fact, he returned to continue doing his own stunts. Ford recalled, 'At one point, the guard throws me into a mine car and, since I'd just come back from back surgery, I had second thoughts about being the throwee.'

This kind of regimen requires considerable stamina and a supple performer, so the newly gammy Ford decided to hire a personal fitness advisor on the set. The final credit scroll even lists 'Physical conditioning for Mr Ford by Body by Jake, Inc., Jake Steinfeld.' On location, Spielberg joined Harrison in his workouts. Producer Marshall recalled: 'While in Sri Lanka, you'd hear this voice bellowing "Okay! Drop and give me fifty – one, two, three . . ." Amazingly enough, there was an old YMCA in Kandy, so Steven and Harrison would go down there and work out two or three times a week. It was the most primitive weight room I'd even seen, with old bar-bells and ancient benches. Incredible!'

Oddly, Harrison has often said that he personally doesn't much bank on the salutory effects of exercise. He once told *Marquee* magazine, 'I don't believe in exercise. I just believe I should rest and not be sore. Stunts are falling off a tall building or crashing a car – something you'd be silly to think aren't going to hurt you the next day. I call it physical acting.'

As important as his 'physical acting' is to the creation of his characters, Ford's subtler nuances are not lost on his audience. The manager of the General Cinema in Dallas, Texas, who has sat through many an Indiana Jones screening, says, 'Whenever he does one of his cliché Indiana Jones faces, the audiences go wild. Ford is the absolute king of facial expressions. That's his acting style.'

One scene in *Temple of Doom* always succeeded in bringing down the house, recalls the manager. 'When the spiked walls of the cave are coming down to crush Indy and Short Round, and Ford screws up his face and yells at this dumb blonde who has been absolutely no help at all and, with an expression of total indignation, "We are going to *die*" – that's the biggest laugh in the movie.' Another favourite scene is one where Ford parodies his famous visual ad-lib from *Raiders*: confronted by *two* burly baddies brandishing broadswords, Indiana Jones coolly reaches for his trusty pistol – only to find his holster empty.

Despite that fact that audiences reacted with delight more than terror to *Indiana Jones and the Temple of Doom*, the graphic violence portrayed in a film intended for a PG rating (Parental Guidance Suggested) – a man being burned alive, not to mention having his heart bloodily ripped from his chest, children being whipped and tortured – led to quite a furore in the press. Although the movie itself was not the first to adopt the PG–13 rating (Not Recommended for Children Under 13) – that dubious honour went to a minor shocker called *Dreamscape* – it was certainly the catalyst that created the new classification. It's hard to say whether the tempest over violence was responsible for a slackening box office, but the gross receipts that started coming in at 25 per cent better than *Raiders of the Lost Ark* – $231 million-plus in the first year – did fall off slightly in succeeding months.

Ford's response to the negative reaction regarding *Doom* violence was typically low-key. 'I do believe that repeated acts of violence inure one to further violence,' he said. 'But in that, I'm talking about *real* violence, where journalists minutely examine an assassination, or revel in the details of a murder.'

Those fans who closed their eyes at the gruesome sequences and stomach-churners like the notorious Bug Banquet, did well to open them for the elaborate stage designs by Elliott Scott, art director for early Hitchcock films. He created sets for the Temple of Doom, the Pleasure Pavilion of the Palace of Pankot and other interiors with: ten thousand yards of sash cord; three thousand sheets of plywood; seven hundred thousand feet of timber; two hundred and fifty tons of plaster; thirty tons of cement; one hundred and sixty yards of sand; five hundred blocks of polystyrene; one thousand sheets of metal lath; three thousand gallons of paint and polish; twenty-five boxes of fibreglass matt; and untold vats of resin.

Ford was once quoted as saying his movie success has 'no magic involved, only work and circumstance.' But some suspect that turning polystyrene and sand into the Pleasure Palace of Pankot does take at least a *little* magic, somewhere along the line.

Chapter Eight

Acting As An Art

'Unlike some actors, I cannot be good in a bad picture,' said Ford. 'Failures are inevitable. And, unfortunately, in film, they live forever and they're forty feet wide and twenty feet high! But that's the price you pay. It's not so easy to pick and choose. What's difficult is to find something that's arousing to both your enthusiasm and your imagination.'

The next part that aroused Harrison's enthusiasm and imagination would be the one to lift him to the level of professional respect he sought, a demanding role that would prove his validity as an actor. 'You might say there's more range in *Witness*, but that's the easy part,' said Ford. 'When you have more range, it's far easier to seduce the audience, because you have more tools to work with. The more limited the character, the greater the challenge. For instance, how much does anyone know about the family background of Indiana Jones?'

Fans who recognized the quality of Ford's work in the little-known *Hanover Street* and *Heroes* would agree with Ford's statement that *Witness* may seem like an advance in complexity in my film roles, but I have been able to do other complex parts as well. They just haven't been as successful artistically or commercially as the other films.'

The plot of *Witness* revolves around an eight-year-old Amish boy (played by eleven-year-old Lukas Haas) who witnesses a drug-related murder in the men's room of a Philadelphia train station. Ford is the big-city cop assigned to the case, who soon realizes that the culprits are his own colleagues. Originally travelling to the witness's Lancaster County farm to solve a murder, he ends up staying there to prevent one – his own. Naturally, a romance develops between the cop and the little boy's widowed mother (Kelly McGillis). And it is this collision of two worlds – that of a 20th-century man to whom violence is an everyday fact of life, and that of a pacifist woman whose society has remained rigidly unchanged since the 18th century – that lifts the story onto a level of interest much higher than its *Starsky and Hutch* outline makes it appear.

It was this compelling mix of clashing cultures, polarized politics, morals and mores than attracted Ford to the project. The fact that this movie has a message – whether he personally believed it or not – made *Witness* something Ford wanted to be a part of. Too seldom these days, he felt, did writers and actors care if they actually communicated anything of substance to the consumers.

'You come away with more of a feeling than a message,' said Ford. 'I don't feel I ever want to make a film without a message. I want to provide people with an experience out of which their corollary experience allows them to have thoughts about it.' (Translation: You can learn something.)

Producer Edward S. Feldman said, 'You're always looking for a story and a background that haven't been done a hundred times before. *Witness* is one of those. This is a movie that has something to say. You go with your instincts.'

Feldman's instincts took him straight to Ford, who responded with an immediate positive answer and began to take an integral part and personal interest in the film. His concern became evident to everyone on the set.

Ford's first significant contribution was in the choice of the film's director. 'Harrison and I felt director Peter Weir [*The Last Wave*, *Year of Living Dangerously*] would bring something unusual to the work,' remembered Feldman. Both felt that an outsider – an Australian, in this case – would bring a fresh perspective to this view of two very different aspects of Americana.

In Weir's unbiased eyes, Ford felt, the Amish view of contemporary America would emerge more clearly, making starker the contrast between their way of life and that of Ford's policeman, John Book. The Amish, who emigrated to America in the 1700s to flee religious persecution – they are Swiss Anabaptists – began their life in the new world in isolation and have maintained that isolation ever since. None have radios, telephones, central heating or automobiles. They go to market in horse-drawn buggies, communicate at community gatherings, and live in a centuries-old style that requires married men to have untrimmed beards (with no moustaches) and uncut hair. Buttons, as was mentioned in the movie, are considered a sign of vanity, and all clothing is fastened with hooks and eyes.

The distance that the Amish maintain between themselves and outsiders posed a problem when it came to hiring extras for the shoot. Normally, film-makers find 'atmosphere' players in the community of a location setting itself. But since the code of the Amish prohibits photographers, this was impossible. A former member of the Amish church did serve as technical director, but Amish co-operation *per se* was limited to one couple who offered to rent their buggies and farm equipment to the production. What curiosity the Amish did have about the cinematic goings-on, they satisfied from a distance, through binoculars.

There were other near-fatal problems. Peter Weir almost had to turn *Witness* down, since he had already signed to direct *Mosquito Coast*, based on Paul Theroux's 1982 novel of the same name. But because *Coast* was having a hell of a time finding enough financing for a green light, Weir was able to slot in *Witness* during his down-time. Filming for *Witness* began in the summer of 1984. Originally, the movie was going to be titled *Called Home*, but Paramount felt that name was a little weak (not to mention a little reminiscent of the *E.T.* tag line). The studio offered a $400 bonus to any corporate employee who could come up with a better handle. The joke went that, thanks to Weir's previous track record, the new movie should be called *The Year of Living Amishly*. (Harrison had his own personal pun for *Witness*. Between takes, he wandered around the set wearing a black t-shirt with white lettering that read 'Indiana Stoltzfus' – Stoltzfus being a traditional Amish surname, as common in Lancaster County as Smith . . . or Jones.)

Even though Weir respected Ford's own track record, he still had to be convinced that the actor could undertake as subtle a portrait as was needed for John Book. If the two hadn't hit it off on a personal level, creative disagreements would have plagued *Witness*. Luckily, the two men got on famously. Weir called Ford 'one of the leading men who have all those qualities that the screen loves. I was interested that Harrison wanted to extend his range. Then, it was a matter of whether we personally got on, which we did right off, because we had similar concerns for the film.'

Ford agreed. 'I never wanted to do just another cop movie. I have great respect for the screenplay. This film has many element, but mostly it's an opportunity to present a kind of experience you can only get in movies. Peter Weir has taken full advantage of that.'

Ford spent more than a month intensively preparing for his role. During two weeks of tutelage with Philadelphia homicide detective Eugene Dooley, Ford observed the workings of a real major crimes unit, and participated in two police raids – one of them serving a warrant on a murder suspect. Recalled Ford, 'All I knew about cops was what I had seen on television and in the movies and, suffice it to say, it ain't like that.'

Ford's own views on the relationship between the law and the public were themselves changed by his experience. 'I held all the liberal predispositions against the use of unreasonable force,' said Ford after his first 'bust,' 'and I came to understand what the value of "up against the wall" was. When these guys kicked in the door and went in, it totally disarmed the people who were inside, to the point where they offered no resistance – which is exactly the idea.'

Witness gave Ford the opportunity also to draw on his real past experiences, and he used his own life to mould the nuances that made John Book a compelling character. It was Ford's idea, for instance, to make John Book a better carpenter in the barn-raising scene than his competition, played by dancer Alexander Godunov – and it was, of course, his own prior career that made it believable. During the shoot, Ford quipped: 'I always knew I could make more than $12.50 an hour doing this!' It was also due to Harrison that one of the movie's best-loved scenes took shape: he suggested the Sam Cooke tune '(What a) Wonderful World' for the romantic dance between himself and Kelly McGillis – having remembered the song fondly from the *American Graffiti* soundtrack.

Co-star McGillis also went through extensive preparation and study for her part as the young widow. First, though, she had to overcome her apprehension about working with Ford – not because she had heard anything bad about the man himself, but because he represented to her the Hollywood Movie Star. McGillis herself had previously appeared in only one film (*Reuben, Reuben*) and was still doing a day job.

Until production began, Kelly was serving snacks at a Greenwich Village coffee house. 'They picked me up at work once, Ford and Weir,' she recalled. 'I wasn't done yet, so I made them wait about twenty minutes. The whole time, everyone is whispering, "Harrison Ford is here!" And then after my shift, I sat down with him and they all said in the cafe, "Who the hell does she think she is, sitting with Harrison Ford?" It was unbelievable. I was very intimidated by him at first, because he's such a star. I discovered that he's just a regular guy. He's just like everybody else. He's not anything to be terrified of, but for a long time, I was very scared of him.'

McGillis honed her character by reading books, watching documentaries about the Amish, and even lived with an Amish family and their seven children for a number of days, to observe and participate in the daily routine. She reported that, 'besides speaking English, they use a lot of words that we don't. What they call Dutch – actually a form of low German – is spoken in the home. The youngest child, a four-year-old, spoke only Dutch, so it was a great learning experience trying to communicate with him.' This particular segment of McGillis's education was cut short, however, when the family's neighbours got wise to her real profession, and she had to flee.

All the study and attention to detail that went into the pre-production of *Witness* paid off in the end. The film made $4,450,000 in its first weekend, and the critics called John Book 'the best role of his [Ford's] career' (Rex Reed). Said *Cosmopolitan*, '*Witness* furnishes Harrison Ford with the perfect vehicle for proving he's more than a mere macho, whip-cracking hipster . . . he couples the surface cool of Indiana Jones with a refreshing, deep-rooted warmth.'

California magazine raved, 'If he weren't already a major star, his role as John Book would make him one.' The *Village Voice* went on at great length, saying in part: 'Although he has shot and lashed and leapt his way through five of the cinema's biggest blockbusters, we still know him as scarcely more than a cartoon charmer glimpsed amid the hurtling special effects of Steven Spielberg and George Lucas. At *Witness* bucolic pace, we have time to contemplate his knobby nose and soft, rounded chin. This ain't such a tough guy. When he isn't squinting like a hardened man of battle, Ford's eyes go goo-goo, and his manner sheepish – he's the movie's other little boy. He's also alert and intelligent; unlike, say, Burt Reynolds, of whom he's the thinking man's equivalent, Ford can mug in character, and when it's time to get serious, he projects convincing concern for young Samuel and affecting ambivalence over his kind and beautiful mother. One expects a superhero and meets, instead, a man.'

At the end of the year, *Witness* was in the running for eight Oscars, and Ford was given the highest honour an actor could aspire to: an Academy Award nomination for Best Performance.

'Well, *Witness* is really acting,' said Ford. 'It's great to get a chance to play a real person. My ambition was to play real people in *Star Wars* and *Raiders*. But doing this movie didn't feel any different from doing any other movie. The process was the same. It was regular acting,' he shrugged. He later added, 'You try to figure out what to do, and then you go out there and do it. If you've figured out what to do, but don't have the craft to do it, you're in trouble. I'm quite happy to be a craftsman.'

Where *Witness* most differed from Ford's earlier roles was not in the film's process, but in its context. The cultural conflicts underlying a tense storyline added a second layer of interaction, a subtext, that lent it a significance it would otherwise have lacked. Imagine what a different movie you would have ended up with had the action concerned a cop moving not from Philadelphia to Lancaster County but from, for example, Detroit to Beverly Hills.

'I don't think of it as a movie having the potential of being more serious than the two adventure series,' Ford said. 'It gave me a certain satisfaction that we were going to be able to make audiences feel something more subtle, more complex, than other things I've done. I like to add something onto a script that already has a good reason for being.' This is why Ford has no desire to see vehicles written with him in mind. 'If something is developed especially for you, you don't put much into it.'

Harrison Ford brought to *Witness* something very personal: his soul. He may call it 'mere' craft, but artifice alone – not matter how expertly realized – can never convey the humanity that Ford imbued in John Book. Said critic Kenneth Turan, 'Ford's work in the likes of *Star Wars* and *Raiders of the Lost Ark*, effective though it was, now has to be considered little more than slumming.'

Chapter Nine

Ford At Home

If you asked Harrison Ford what the two biggest prices he had to pay for his stardom were, he'd answer: his first marriage, and his privacy. He is perhaps the most closed-mouth star in the Hollywood constellation (now that Garbo has moved away), and has made almost a game of revealing nothing truly personal about himself in more than a decade's worth of probing newspaper and magazine interviews. 'I'm not willing to absolutely gift-box myself up and say, ''This is the puzzle, no pieces are missing,'' ' he told *GQ* magazine last year. In the Harrison Ford puzzle, almost every piece is missing; the picture has to be extrapolated at every angle. In his lifelong effort to remain ordinary, Harrison Ford has become all but invisible. 'I've characterized myself as a private person, and not only are people now willing to accept that, in fact it feels better to them.'

Ford absolutely insists on remaining all but anonymous, no matter how well known his features. He avoids interviews, glamour bashes and celebrity-studded screenings at any cost. 'I live in fear of being stuck at some Hollywood party for eternity,' Ford once told journalist Craig Modderno. 'You'd only find me in a disco if I died and didn't go to heaven.' To Harrison Ford, acting is a job like any other. 'I'm not complicated or mysterious,' he said. 'I just do my job, and am lucky to be in efficient, entertaining pictures. We have fun making them, but we never thought they'd be monster hits.'

Ford is reluctant to talk about anything but acting and its role in his life; the best sense of the man we can really get is through his work. But the way in which he perceives a role and his obligation to the public – and how that relates to his view of society and its impact on him – is telling.

'I guess I worry about society almost neurotically,' he said, 'though I don't do anything practical like stocking my basement with emergency provisions. Civilization is at a point where our concerns seem to be how less to harm people than how to make them any better, and I find that fairly depressing. It wouldn't help for me to become some kind of martyr, pleading to a crowd to avoid this or embrace that; actors who get up and do that, and fans who expect it, are really misinterpreting a performer's job. We're in another branch of public service – we're assistant story-tellers, not role models or pontiffs of morality and logic.'

This theory explains why Ford seldom reveals his personal views on religion, politics or sexual mores. He doesn't want the folks out there to take his opinion as being in any way superior to their own, some kind of gospel from the mount, simply because he represents to them the infallible Han Solo or Indiana Jones. Ford wants everyone to separate his own views from those of his characters – and the easiest way to do that is not to give them his own views in the first place. The sole purpose to which he puts his notoriety is to promote his films. He told *DramaLogue*: 'I don't do much publicity in my own cause. I think people only have so much interest in anybody, and if you barrage them in between times you have something to offer them, you become a personality rather than an actor. And I'm not interested in that.'

The Ford desire for privacy extends right down to street level. Jan Jackson, Ford's Beverly Hills neighbour for two years, says 'I still don't know what he's like. I never went inside his home. He's a very, very private person.'

Harrison Ford finds it vital to his sanity to draw a line between 'person' and 'personality.' In an interview with *Celebrity Register*, he stated, 'The natural state for an actor is that of observer, where you can learn something. Instead, I'm the focus of attention. When you're written about, you're stuck with a "personality" – even if it's your own.'

Talking to writer Kenneth Turan years later, he expanded, 'You're disadvantaged as an actor by becoming the observed rather than being an observer. If your life changes so much that you're no longer able to have mundane experiences, then your personality's going to undergo an inevitable shift that's not going to be appropriate to the work you do. So you've got to protect yourself. It makes it *more* necessary to have a normal life, to invest yourself in real things.'

The Ford reticence continues – unfortunately, he admits – right down to personal relationships. He once said that he was difficult to live with because he keeps his thoughts to himself. (He's also said he's difficult to live with because he's so detail-oriented, judgemental and demanding.) In a way, he has merged his true-life self with that of his Resourceful Man characters: it is self-reliant Harrison Ford who has to come to Harrison Ford's rescue. Although he adores his friends and family, he doesn't exercise one of the main prerogatives of close personal relationships – that of burdening them with any of his problems.

Said Ford, 'I just don't go to anyone for advice or for a shoulder to lean on. My questions are for me to answer out of my own experience. The Buddha said, "work out your salvation with diligence." '

Ford simply insists on keeping his personal

salvation separate from any mere professional objectives. 'The most interesting thing about me is the work that I do,' he continually – and, some observers snipe, all too accurately – repeats. He told the *Chicago Tribune* in 1982, 'I don't particularly like to talk. I'm not a big talker – I mean, a yakker.' (That line was repeated in perhaps four other interviews the same year. Imagine getting that much mileage out of saying nothing!) To another newspaper reporter, he said, 'There are a lot more interesting people to talk to than me. I guarantee it. I haven't allowed people to get an angle on me.'

Whether his college sweetheart Mary hadn't been able to get an angle on Ford either, or whether a combination of frustrating emotional isolation and constant separations caused by work finally brought about the split, Ford's first marriage ended in 1978. Mary had often visited Ford on location, but these temporary reunions proved inadequate to hold a marriage together, much less a family. Ironically, this personal failure occurred during the period just after *Star Wars* when film offers arrived in every mail, and Harrison and Mary were at long last able to count the rewards after years of paying dues.

Ford was desolate that his marriage couldn't be salvaged. He was brought up to believe that marriage should last forever, as has that of his parents, and that it should never be a decision hastily made. It would be another five years before he attempted marriage again.

Ford's two sons, Ben and Willard, were in their pre-teens when their parents broke up in 1978, but Ford believes that the experience has not adversely affected his sons' feelings towards him. It was not yet another clichéd Tinseltown split; 'glamour life claims yet another casualty.' And the reason for that is quite simple, claims Harrison: the boys were born long before Daddy was a star. During their early childhoods, Ford worked at other things besides acting, and did well at them. The boys found it easy, therefore, to accept his career as just that – a well-paying job that he happens to be good at.

'Having a star as a dad hasn't changed their lives,' Ford said. Asked point-blank about his children, he told an interviewer: 'I don't want to drag them into this,' and he never has. Certainly, each son went on to lead a pretty normal life. Ben, 19, inclines towards Indiana Jones-style feats of athletics, maintaining an impressive .666 batting average for his high school team before enrolling as a student at the University of Southern California. Willard, 17, lives like most Southern California teens with disposable income in their designer jeans. He won't say a word about his father. (Some fellow USC students will hint that young Ben Ford has been known to pull a 'Don't you know who I am?' routine upon occasion, but quickly draws back to blend in with the crowd.)

Oddly enough, despite his fame, Harrison Ford often escapes notice himself, because of his ordinary boyish looks. 'If I find the word "handsome'' in a script, I'll run away,' he once laughed. He describes himself as having a 'kind of plastic' face. A *Life* magazine spread last year featured a picture of Ford and his new wife, screenwriter Melissa Mathison (*Black Stallion*, *E.T.*) standing in a Philadelphia crowd – unnoticed. The amazing thing is that Ford didn't hide behind sunglasses, pull a hat low over his face or conceal himself in a bulky coat. He wore a sports jacket and trousers and looked exactly like – Harrison Ford. Mary too wore a simple outfit: perhaps the very down-to-earthiness of their appearance 'hid' them from a public that expects its stars to be dazzlingly larger-than-life. Ford said, 'They're looking for Indiana Jones, so people can't recognize me sometimes . . . and sometimes they can. I can go for days without anyone recognizing me. There's nothing really striking about my physiognomy. [Except for that Laguna Beach-era scar, for the eagle-eyed observer.] I lead a pretty normal life, and I don't go out in public very much because I don't want to.'

Ford met Mathison, eight years his junior, through the charmed circle of Lucas–Spielberg–Coppola. Her first major screenplay was produced by Francis Ford; her second by Steven. Harrison and Melissa married in 1983. From the time the pair starting dating, thoughts of the two collaborating on a movie buzzed in the brains that give birth to box-office bonanzas. How could a big time screenwriter partnered with a big time star miss? Ford, however, doesn't have any intention of bringing the office into the bedroom. 'I don't take my work home with me at all.'

'We're helpful to each other's careers, but we don't have any intention of working together,' he said in a recent interview. 'We each keep to our own track.'

There is no question, however, that occasional runs on the other's tracks have been beneficial, particularly in Mathison's case. Melissa accompanied the crew for *Raiders of the Lost Ark* from time to time to their various locations. During the course of the production, she and producer Kathleen Kennedy became friendly. Melissa's *Black Stallion* ranked as one of Kennedy's favourite movies; when Kennedy's boss, Steven Spielberg, had the idea for *E.T.* and needed someone to write the screenplay for it, Kennedy suggested Melissa.

Spielberg said he'd 'give it some thought,' and one evening, while Melissa ate dinner, Steven sauntered over and pitched her the story. 'I essentially pitched the simple premise, and she loved it,' Spielberg recalls. Mathison remembers differently, stating that she said, 'Thank you very much, but I've just decided never to write another page again. I read what I had written in England, and hated it.'

Undaunted, Spielberg persisted, approaching Melissa again and again when the shoot moved to Tunisia. Melissa related, 'One day, Steven and I were searching for scorpions, turning over rocks, and he brought it up.' By this time, she had warmed to the idea, but felt 'I couldn't mention it until he asked me again.' Ask he did, and she began writing what was first called 'A Boy's Life' on October 8, 1980, producing a preliminary draft script in eight weeks.

'I would work for a week, and then go down and meet Steven in the Marina del Rey, where he was editing *Raiders*, and show him what I had and talk about it. And I'd go home and work a week, and come back and meet him again. And the story just kind of evolved.'

Spielberg called the script 'one of the best first drafts I've ever read.' And the finished product was good enough to win Melissa the Writers Guild of America award for Best Screenplay.

E.T. began shooting in September, 1981. The box-office gross of $360 million makes it one of the six all-time highest grossing movies in history – and had Harrison Ford and Melissa Mathison appeared in the film as was intended, Ford would have the distinction of having been in all six.

It happened like this: originally, screenwriter Mathison was to take a cameo role in *E.T.*, playing a school nurse in the scene where child star Henry Thomas's character Elliott becomes drunk and disorderly in class. Ford was to walk on in the guise of the school principal. But Melissa, it turned out, is as camera-shy as her husband is publicity-shy. During the filming, her hands literally shook with fear as she tried to pull off the small role. The two scenes in which she and Harrison appeared had to be clipped, and ended up on the infamous cutting room floor.

Harrison and Melissa, when they're not involved in a mega-movie project, have a choice of places to hide. They have a home in Santa Monica, constructed from the ground up under the watchful eye of the ex-carpenter, a place in the Caribbean, and a retreat in Wyoming. Another home in Beverly Hills was recently sold.

Although Harrison says that half the furniture in Los Angeles attributed to him was built by either Ethan Alan or Levitz – and that he seldom has time these days to swing a hammer – he still does construct some special pieces for his own house. When he does buy furniture, he is as scrupulous and detail-minded as you would imagine. He and Melissa frequent one antique shop in West Hollywood reserved for professional decorators, the Richard Mulligan Shop, and co-owner Mollie Mulligan noted that 'When Harrison Ford buys a piece of furniture, he turns it over to see how it's constructed. He wants to make sure he's buying quality.' Ford developed a passion for Amish and Shaker woodwork after completing *Witness*, and the Mulligan shop specializes in the genre.

Harrison Ford once told *Time* magazine that he drives 'a red car and a black car,' and that was as much about his personal life as he wanted to reveal. Actually, Ford drives a 911 SC Porsche Targa, and sold a 380 SEL Mercedes in favour of a 733 BMW. And he did go to Electronic Entertainment Inc. – known as 'The Car Stereo Store of the Stars' – to have top-of-the-line sound systems and intruder alarms installed, at a cost of about $3,500 per vehicle. The Los Angeles-based firm is famed for a client roster that includes the King of Saudi Arabia, Elizabeth Taylor, the Sultan of Oman, Burt Reynolds, Lionel Richie, Mr T and many more.

Electronic Entertainment owner and president Howard Becker, who became friendly with Ford as he supervised the work on his vehicles, describes Harrison as 'a little reserved. He's not flamboyant and he's somewhat serious, not a joker. He's certainly meticulous. At one point, he was showing me the way to put something in mechanically on a particular stereo installation, and he got really involved in it. He had a good eye, too. I kidded him – I told him he could work here on Saturdays. And he's good enough, to say the least.'

Ford took the jest with equanimity, but he is not what one would call a pushover as a customer. 'He's easy enough to work with,' says Becker, 'but he is demanding. He doesn't get emotional and upset if things go wrong, but he's not at all forgiving when something's late or not working quite right.

'I think he must be wonderful for producers and directors to work with, because he's not putty – he's a strong individual who will let you know what his opinions are and what he feels is best. He's his own man. As a manager, I can state that he would make an excellent manager.' And as a BA in psychology, Becker's observations are not made lightly.

Becker admired Ford's musical tastes – ranging widely, they run to jazz and new age innovators – and liked to make fun of the house the actor was then living in. 'He didn't have all the garage room in the world, so two of the cars would normally be left outside, and there were large trees on the cul de sac where he lived. So the cars always looked dirty, which was definitely not in line with his usual habits of maintenance.'

Ford was never one to throw his weight around, and no kind of a braggart. But his quiet assurance would still peek through. 'Because I work with a lot of producers and directors,' says Becker, 'like Sydney Pollack, Mark Rydell, Joe Silver and others, and I hear their side of things all the time, I asked Harrison "Who calls the shots, them or you?" And he looks at me and says "Nobody calls the shots for me any more." It was a simple statement, but he said it with a real gleam in his eye. He's as happy as anybody would be who'd reached that point in his career. He's respected for his talent and his position in life; he's a personality and somebody to be reckoned with. He's real proud of those accomplishments, and I don't blame him.'

Much as Ford likes Becker, he might rankle at the latter's choice of the word 'personality.' It's a term Ford tries to get as far away from as possible – as far as Snake River, Wyoming, where the eternal Hollywood party is just another nightmare.

'It represents an opportunity for me to have a second life, as it were,' Ford said of his ranch. 'Being part of another community whose concerns are different than the concerns of Hollywood. Mostly, it's some place I can go to be alone.'

Ford says he likes to hang out with the guys from the Fish and Game Department, shovel snow off his driveway, and run into town to hit the cleaners or the market just like anyone else. The fact that he could swing by the bank and deposit a cool million in petty cash isn't something he likes to remind his neighbours.

And the Fords have been good neighbours in Wyoming. They were concerned that the wildlife habitat surrounding their homestead could be replaced by cement and buildings, so they put 132 acres in the Western Wyoming Jackson Hole Land Trust to prevent that from happening. Their Snake River property is home to bald eagles, red-tailed hawks, moose, elk, deer and trumpeter swans. The bald eagles and the trumpeter swans are already on the endangered species list, and Harrison and Melissa want to make sure that the others don't end up there as well. 'It's hard to imagine such a place covered with buildings,' said the executive director of the land trust, 'but that could have happened some day. The Fords have done a splendid thing making sure that it never will.'

From defender of Galactic democracy to defender of Wyoming wildlife, Harrison Ford always seems to emerge as the quintessential white hat. He carries his prestige and power with grace, and earns his pay-cheque. 'Ten years ago,' he said in 1984, 'I couldn't have handled this degree of success and money. Now, I simply ask for a certain amount of money and I get it.' His secret of success is simple: 'Persistence. I don't give up easily.'

Harrison and Melissa are considered one of the happiest couples in the industry. The tabloids report that Mrs Ford is expecting Harrison's third child in January, 1987. And that's something he looks forward to: 'Raise more kids, look forward to life on the ranch. I'm slowly trying to transfer stock to my personal life and make sure that I still have some years left for that.' Never again will home be sacrificed on the altar of career.

The next question for Harrison Ford is, in which direction will his persistence lead him now? At 44, is it time for him to leave his swash-buckling days behind, graduate from thinking-man's Burt Reynolds to the next Sean Connery? For his next big-screen assignment, the man in the white hat chose a role that shows him, in Ford's words, 'cantankerous and difficult and a fair share of unsympathetic.'

Chapter Ten

Looking Ahead

As this book goes to press, Harrison Ford takes his riskiest career step since knocking on Sergio Mendes' door with a blank carpentry resumé in hand. *The Mosquito Coast*, released in November 1986, reunites Ford with director Peter Weir, it's true, but in every other way is *terra incognita* for both the actor and his fans. For once, Harrison Ford is no kind of a hero.

This film project has had a long and chequered history. It is based on the 1982 novel of the same name by Paul Theroux, best known for such travel books as *The Great Railway Bazaar* and *The Kingdom by the Sea*. Screen rights to the novel were bought that same year for $250,000 by producer Jerome Hellman (*Coming Home*, *Midnight Cowboy*). 'Very rarely do you read something that gets you really excited,' said Hellman at the time.

111

'I felt it could make a wonderful movie if the right people were involved.'

Hellman hired top screenwriter Paul Schrader (*Taxi Driver*, *Raging Bull*) to turn the book into a script, and the screenplay was ready as early as 1983. Having seen and admired *Picnic at Hanging Rock* and *The Year of Living Dangerously*, Hellman immediately tagged Peter Weir as the director of his choice. 'The thematic harmony between Peter's previous work and *The Mosquito Coast* was striking,' said Hellman. The two met in Australia, and then Hellman brought Weir to New England to scout for locations and meet Theroux. 'Peter was apprehensive,' recalled Hellman. 'He had just had a terrible experience with the novelist of one of his earlier films.' But Theroux told director Weir: 'Take it.' He gave advice and encouragement to the Australian, adding personal insights into his work but never dominating the film-makers' concepts. Theroux once wrote a note to Weir about the character of protagonist Allie Fox, whom Harrison Ford would eventually portray: 'I think the key to Allie,' said Thereoux, 'is showing all sides of his personality and, at times, showing how one lies just beneath the other – loud bullying being a feature of a rather inward shyness, bravery being a wilder manifestation of blind cowardice, and most inventiveness being self-serving.'

Swashbuckling Indiana Jones portraying blind cowardice? Self-effacing Han Solo characterized by loud bullying? But Harrison said that the first time he saw the script, 'I felt, I can play this. [Allie Fox] is complicated, he's f---ing complicated. I *love* that!' He later expanded for interviewer Bob Strauss, 'Allie is a complicated person, and it's a complicated job for the audience to figure him out. He's a good father and a bad father. He's a monster, a clown, a fool, a genius. It was necessary always to preserve enough compassion for him so the audience could understand why he does the things he does.'

Weir recalled, 'I've never had a character like Allie in my films before, that I like and dislike in equal measure. Men like Allie have obviously changed the course of the world's history in certain instances – they've become great statesmen or great dictators. They have a cause and if people must suffer for that cause, then that must be the price.'

Allie Fox is a particular American type, not terribly unlike Ford's familiar Resourceful Man construct but carried to the extreme, over the edge of all reason. Employed as a handyman in Massachusetts but preoccupied with his tinkerings as an inventor, Fox dreams of taking his wife and family away from the threat of nuclear annihilation and the everyday indignities of Western civilization. He dreams of a life uncorrupted by the modern world, a place where an independent man can stand on his own two feet and carve out a future for his loved ones. He packs up his wife, two sons and twin daughters, boards a freighter for the Mosquito Coast (a strip of Central America that extends from Guatemala to Panama, but represented in the film by Belize) and calls out: 'Goodbye, America, and have a nice day!'

Landing in this brave new world of subtropical jungle, Fox buys a 'town' – a collection of tumbledown shacks and weeds – to be turned into a thriving ice-making factory by the sweat of his brow. His family is devastated, although they follow him loyally, through horrendous trials and tribulations. Attacks by ferocious tribes, typhoons, fire – nothing can deter Fox from his goal, and his obsession spirals to madness and tragedy.

This is not upbeat fare, and it is unsurprising that the project didn't find immediate acceptance with the major film studios. It is surprising, though – considering the heavyweight credentials of those involved – that it met with as much resistance as it did. 'We were turned down everywhere,' Hellman told *GQ* magazine, 'most places three or four times.'

The script was originally developed at Warner Bros., but was soon passed over to Britain's Goldcrest. Then it went to Embassy, and then to 20th Century-Fox. 'It was a period when every studio was going through management changes,' said Hellman. 'No sooner had an executive approved it for production then he or she headed elsewhere, leaving Peter and me shopping for another home.' By early 1984, the director and producer realized that it would be at least another year before they could begin shooting, because of the seasonal demands of the plot.

The delay turned out to be kismet, however: Weir was offered *Witness*, which introduced him to Harrison Ford and, in the end, made him a bankable director. And Jack Nicholson, who was the first actor considered for the role of Allie, went on to make *Terms of Endearment*, a role that won him an Oscar. Ironically, the cavalier astronaut in *Terms* was first offered to Ford, who turned it down – knowing that it was Oscar-bait, but still feeling it wasn't right for him. By the time everyone got back to *The Mosquito Coast*, Nicholson was out and Harrison Ford was in.

The moment *Witness* opened to rave reviews, the 'new Ford/Weir project' became a hot property. All the studios that had turned it down the year before were now hard on Hellman's heels, but Hellman decided to seek independent financing and maintain creative control. Producer Saul Zaentz *(One Flew Over the Cuckoo's Nest, Amadeus)* read the script and immediately offered to finance it, for what Hellman said was 'in the low 20 millions. We closed the deal in one day in early March,' recalled the producer, 'and started work on the next.' Ironically enough, the film eventually (and circuitously) ended up in the distribution arms of Warner Bros., the company that had had it in the first place.

Harrison was enthralled at being offered the chance to portray Allie Fox, and never doubted for a moment that he was up to it. 'I don't have any trouble representing something that I understand,' he said, 'and this is a character that I've never felt any difficulty understanding. So I don't think of it as a more difficult job than what I'd done before. On the other hand, I was aware that there was opportunity here for more complicated characterization, and because the character is so verbal and effusive, it goes against the kind of characters for which I'm best known. That was the attraction the part held for me: to do something different.'

Director Weir was also enthralled: 'Harrison Ford was born with the kind of talent that cannot be learned. Combined with the craft that he has mastered over the years, it makes for an extremely potent force.' The combination of Weir and Ford together is also a potent force, a case of the whole being greater than the sum of its parts. We already know full well that Harrison Ford prefers – insists, when he can – to add as much creative input to a film as is humanly possible. Peter Weir is one of the few directors who actually encourages that. Cast-mates remember the pair always being off in some corner during the shoot, talking over one aspect of the script or other. And the talks were not always whispered, either.

'We provoke each other,' said Weir. 'It's no cosy fireside chat, two old colonels agreeing. There's healthy friction; we both have extremely strong opinions.' Claimed Ford, 'We have a lot of fun. There's a real spontaneous flow of ideas. And it seems that there's some mysterious continuity of experience between us that's not biography. I feel a sureness and support of the ideas I'm going for when I work with Peter.' Later, he added, 'We question one another, test and expand each other's notions, and stop the other one when we think he's wrong.'

While the *Coast* shoot wasn't fraught with the dangers of avalanche or elephant rides, it wasn't a complete breeze either. Producer Hellman had decided to use the Central American nation of Belize (formerly British Honduras) some years before, on the recommendation of Norman Jewison, who shot *The Dogs of War* there a decade earlier. A crew composed of Australians, Americans, Britons and Canadians spent from March to July in the company of indigenous boa constrictors (as opposed to imported ones) and shared horror stories of cuts, bruises, mosquito bites (naturally) and sunburn. 'To actually experience the heat, the bugs, the mud and the rain,' said Helen Mirren, who plays Ford's long-suffering on-screen wife, 'was a million times better than playing it on a studio backlot with a few palm trees.' To ease the pain, the cast and crew brought with them: two dozen VCRs and a wide selection of tapes, an elaborate stereo system, four computers, and a capuccino machine. Bagels were flown in regularly from Miami.

'After a while, you just get used to it,' said Ford of yet another exotic location. 'It just becomes part of the job. One of the great disappointments in my life, though, is that I go to these fascinating places, but don't have very much time to see them.'

After pick-up shots in Georgia, it was time to piece the film into a cohesive whole. The vital ingredient in *Mosquito Coast*, everyone realized, was the central character of Allie Fox. And while the weight of responsibility for the performance rested on Ford's shoulders, the final result was also very much a function of direction and editing. In fact, an early cut of the movie was rejected by Jerome Hellman because it wasn't 'tough enough' – Fox came out as a 'likeable eccentric,' his edges softened and his madness diluted into mere quirkiness. This may have made for a more commercially acceptable movie, but it was not the vision of either Hellman or Ford. 'It turned out to be a different movie than the one we imagined – funnier, more emotional, more complex,' Ford commented when he saw the finished product. And he was not afraid of being a bad guy for once.

'Harrison is very courageous,' said young actor River Phoenix (*Explorers, Stand By Me*), who plays Allie Fox's eldest son. 'I think his performance is going to shock a lot of people.'

'I wanted to go as far as I could to the edge, beyond the limits of comfort on occasion,' said Harrison. Was the public ready for such an about-face from their hero? 'Well, if they're diehard fans, then they know it's always been my ambition to change from one role to another, to do a variety of different things,' Ford told *Enter-*

tainment Tonight. 'I think it's worth the ride. I think that the film itself is dealing with serious issues on the face of it, and an adventure story with a fast-paced plot. There is, as they say, something for everybody there.'

In fact, not everybody fell in love with *The Mosquito Coast.* Ford knew he was taking big risks, and many of his fears were correct. Roger Ebert, film critic for TV's *Siskel & Ebert & Movies,* said: '*The Mosquito Coast* is a very hard movie to like. I could appreciate the good acting here, and I could admire the way Harrison Ford allowed his character's insanity to take over, [but] it was so clear that this man was not a visionary, not a mystic, but simply nuttier than a fruitcake. The hero's bizarre behaviour kept me on the outside looking in.'

Ebert's partner/antagonist, Gene Siskel, was rather warmer towards the film. 'I found myself on the inside with him,' he said, 'because in the beginning, I didn't think he was nuttier than a fruitcake. This guy seriously thinks there are problems in the land, and wants to do something about it. It reminded me of the Sixties notion of making it a better world . . . This movie is quite compelling in showing that descent into madness out of good intentions. The movie is about how noble wishes and noble desires can be misled.' And, he noted, 'the acting was great.'

Competing syndicated film critic Rex Reed adored the movie, predicting a fresh round of Oscar nominations for both Weir and Ford. Reed called it 'one of the most important films of the year . . . an exhilarating, pulse-pounding film of excitement and originality.' Reed's co-host, Bill Harris, added that it was 'Harrison Ford's best role ever . . . a wonderful film.'

In taking this chance, adopting the persona of a potentially hateful man, Harrison Ford won in one respect: his acting was universally showered with praise. Observers who didn't already perceive the depth and breadth of his talent after *Blade Runner* and *Witness* were now convinced that this was no cardboard *poseur*, but a performer of undeniable skill and feeling. On a commercial level, though, the bet may have turned out to be a loser. The first weekend grosses at the box office were a mere $110,313 – a drop in the bucket compared to a *Star Wars*. It should be noted, however, that the film opened in an extremely limited release, playing in only three theatres nationwide at the outset.

The performance was appreciated, but the movie as a whole left many cold. As *Time* magazine put it, 'though Harrison Ford offers a hypnotizing portrayal of a man covering despair with lunatic optimism, hysteria with bravado and rigid self-control, a fatal prejudice lingers in the audience: we do not want to spend a couple of hours with Allie any more than we would if he were, heaven forfend, our next-door neighbour.'

The *Wall Street Journal*, of all people, took exception to Ford once again drawing upon his resources as a former builder to flesh out footage of the Fox family trying to construct their fantasyland. 'There are far too many scenes,' wrote Julie Salamon, 'of Mr Ford (in real life once a carpenter) sawing and welding. Both here and in *Witness*, Mr Weir has fixated on the sight of Mr Ford working, as though to remind us of the spiritual rewards of physical labour – prized especially by those who don't do it.'

That's rather a pat remark directed at Ford, who still finds solace in physical labour as well as isolation from progress at his Snake River retreat. Allie Fox isn't *that* different from Harrison Ford – it's just that Harrison Ford has come to terms with his personal obsessions, and is in general a nicer guy. Ford himself admitted to the *Los Angeles Herald Examiner* that there are many points at which he and Allie connect. 'I'm a father and a son, so I can recognize the dynamics of that relationship. I'm a person who has worked with his hands, so I can understand that part of it. And I don't accept things the way they are, so I can relate to his criticisms of how American life has come to be. There's no lack of understanding between myself and Allie Fox. It's really a matter of degree: he goes much further than I might go.'

Devoted as Ford was to *The Mosquito Coast*, it did have its cost. The shoot was still in full swing when he was offered a plum part – not to mention a four million dollar salary – in Richard Attenborough's *Biko*, the life story of South Africa's anti-apartheid martyr, Steven Biko. As an actor who always looks for some underlying message in the films he undertakes, Ford was particularly drawn to this important cause.

'There has to be some ambition, some goal the film aspires to,' said Ford. 'I'm fuelled by ideas. If I don't have ideas to reference to, I don't have any way of managing my invention.'

Harrison has been offered $10 million to take on the long-batted-about project set in the world of bicycle racing, 'Yellow Jersey'. The picture has been bounced from studio to studio, star to star (Dustin Hoffman was expected to make it for some time) but there's still no word on a production date – if any.

Ford also mentioned that he wouldn't turn down the role of playwright Harvey Fierstein's gay lover in a screen adaptation of the award-winning play, *Torch Song Trilogy*. (Fierstein, however, told *People* magazine he'd prefer to see Richard Chamberlain play the part, thanks.) So far, no go-ahead has been given for this production, either.

We do know that a script for the next Indiana Jones epic is already in the draft stage, and that Harrison Ford, his trilby and his bullwhip will be back for at least one more heart-stopping adventure.

As an actor who never again has to worry whether or not he'll have enough work to feed his family, Ford is in the position of being able to pick and choose parts that say something to him – he has the freedom *not* to work if he chooses. Spending time with his wife and (soon to be) new family on his Wyoming retreat is now more important than seeing his name in lights. It took a long time to reach that point, perhaps – the point where all the hard work to carve out a name in Hollywood for himself was just preparation for the ability to turn his back on it. But, as always, Harrison Ford will persevere and persevere to attain his chosen goal. Ain't that gonna be the best damn ranch on the prairie!

Appendix

Harrison Ford Filmography

THEATRICAL MOTION PICTURES

Dead Heat on a Merry-Go-Round (Columbia
    Pictures, 1966)

Luv (Columbia Pictures, 1967)

A Time For Killing, a.k.a. *Long Ride Home*
    (Columbia Pictures, 1967)

Zabriskie Point (Universal Pictures, 1969)

Getting Straight (Universal Pictures, 1970)

American Graffiti (Universal Pictures, 1973)

The Conversation (Paramount Pictures, 1974)

Star Wars (Twentieth Century-Fox, 1977)

Heroes (Universal Pictures, 1977)

Force Ten From Navarone (American International
    Pictures, 1978)

Hanover Street (Paramount Pictures, 1979)

Apocalypse Now (United Artists, 1979)

More American Graffiti (Universal Pictures, 1979)

The Frisco Kid (Warner Brothers, 1979)
The Empire Strikes Back (LucasFilm/Twentieth
    Century–Fox, 1980)
Raiders of the Lost Ark (Paramount Pictures, 1981)
Blade Runner (Warner Brothers, 1982)
Return of the Jedi (LucasFilm/Twentieth
    Century-Fox, 1983)
Indiana Jones and the Temple of Doom (Paramount
    Pictures, 1984)
Witness (Paramount Pictures, 1985)
Mosquito Coast (Warner Brothers, 1986)

TELEVISION MOVIES
The Possessed
The Court Martial of Lt. Calley
Dynasty
Journey to Shiloh

EPISODIC TELEVISION
FBI
Dan August
Gunsmoke
Ironside
Love, American Style
My Friend Tony
Kung Fu

About the Authors

Ethlie Ann Vare is an entertainment journalist whose previous books include biographies of Stevie Nicks and Ozzy Osbourne. Her latest work is *Mothers of Invention: Great Creative Women in History*, a tribute to female inventors and discoverers. Her two weekly newspaper columns, 'Video Beat' and 'Rock on TV', are syndicated to 1,700 newspapers in the US and Canada, and she can also be read in such publications as *Billboard*, *Countdown*, *Pulse*, *In Fashion* and the *New York Times*. She lives in Los Angeles, where she is currently working on a history of Hollywood stuntmen.

Mary Toledo is a Los Angeles-based freelance writer who specializes in rock music. She has written for such publications as *Creem Metal*, *Faces Rocks*, *Rock Scene* and *Music Connection*. She is a graduate of Los Angeles Valley College in journalism and plans to start a rock and roll magazine of her own some day.